# THE HISTORY OF

# CHURCHILL AND SARSDEN

# THE HISTORY OF

# CHURCHILL AND SARSDEN

*The Earth and the Empire:*

*Birthplace of William Smith and Warren Hastings*

**Ralph Mann**

**Churchill Old Church Preservation Society**

© Ralph Mann, 2013

Published by    Churchill Old Church Preservation Society
                Birchwood
                The Sidings
                Churchill
                OX7 6ND

A CIP catalogue record for this book is available from the British Library.

ISBN 978-0-9575690-0-3

Book and cover layout & design by Clare Brayshaw

Photograph on back cover by Richard Kendal

Prepared and printed by:

York Publishing Services Ltd
64 Hallfield Road
Layerthorpe
York YO31 7ZQ

Tel: 01904 431213

Website: www.yps-publishing.co.uk

# DEDICATION

For the people of Churchill,
where our children went happily to school.

# CONTENTS

# ILLUSTRATIONS

# CHURCHILL OLD CHURCH PRESERVATION SOCIETY

In the early 1980s Churchill Old Church, the last medieval building in the village, was made redundant. It was still used for funeral services but at the time it was in poor repair. The Oxford Diocese indicated it might demolish the church. Dr Russell Rathbone, who lived in Hastings House, formed a small committee to preserve the Old Church and the committee established the Churchill Old Church Preservation Society. It was restored so effectively that in 1988 the Privy Council ordered it to be vested in the care of the Oxford Diocesan Board of Finance. However, since then, it has been maintained by the Society which was registered as a charity in 1992. In determining a use for the Old Church, it subsequently founded the much-commended Churchill and Sarsden Heritage Centre.

www.churchillheritage.org.uk

# REVD RALPH MANN

Ralph Mann was born in 1927 and was educated at St John's School, Leatherhead, and at Brasenose College, Oxford. After graduating in Modern History, he taught in Broadstairs, Manchester, Barbados, Bristol City Museum and Sierra Leone. From 1963-1973 he was Head of History at Kingham Hill School, and from 1973-1982 at Chipping Norton School. He was ordained in the Church of England in 1982, and served in the Diocese of Gloucester. He retired in 2000 and lives in Hook Norton.

Churchill circa 1766

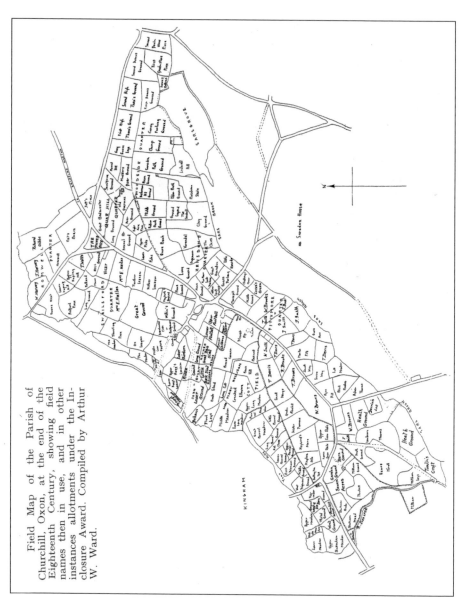

Field Map of the Parish of Churchill, Oxon, at the end of the Eighteenth Century, showing field names then in use, and in other instances allotments under the Inclosure Award. Compiled by Arthur W. Ward.

*Field map post-Enclosure*

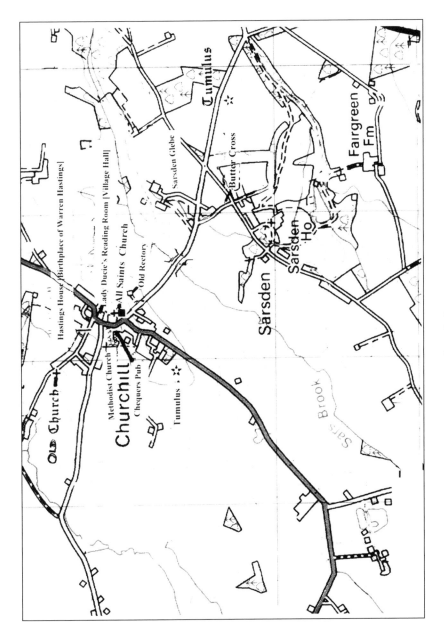

Churchill 2012

# THE STORY OF CHURCHILL PARISH

It is now nearly eighty years since the late Mrs Lilian E. Rose published 'The History of Churchill` in the excellent series promoted by the Oxford Federation of Women's Institutes. Copies of Mrs Rose's book are now very hard to obtain, and, when available second-hand, are extremely expensive. So the time has perhaps come to approach this subject from a slightly different angle, while acknowledging all the research and hard work that Mrs Rose and her helpers undertook. I have therefore tried to avoid repeating the information in Mrs Rose's book.

No attempt to rewrite the history of Churchill would be complete without an acknowledgment of the extensive research by the late Neil Bromwich. Sadly, he was unable to publish before he died, and his records have been dispersed.

This present study began life as a history of the parish of Churchill – its church and its clergy. In an attempt to reach a wider interest I have included several sections relating to the village, its people and their daily lives. Also, when writing about Churchill, it would be absurd to omit reference to its best-known sons, Warren Hastings and William Smith, as well as to some of its more colourful Lords of the Manor.

However, one needs to remember what an important part the church in the past played in the everyday lives of ordinary people. The parson was one of the most highly respected members of the community, and at times when the lord of the manor was a remote figure the vicar was the dominant personality in the parish. To present the church in a strong light is to provide a balanced picture of a village history.

The story of a small north Oxfordshire village may seem a trivial contribution to the overall history of the nation, but our nation's magnificent record is composed of such stories. As Thomas Gray meditated in his Elegy in Stoke Poges churchyard, the unrecorded lives of countless individuals are to be as valued as those of kings, generals, prime ministers or bishops:

> Full many a flower is born to blush unseen
> And waste its sweetness on the desert air.
>
> Some village Hampden, that with dauntless breast
> The little tyrant of his fields withstood,
> Some mute inglorious Milton here may rest,
> Some Cromwell, guiltless of his country's blood.

**Ralph Mann**

**April, 2012**

# BEGINNINGS

It is difficult to pass through this district without noticing the elegant tower of Churchill church in its commanding hill-top position. Few tourists discover the neighbouring churches at Cornwell or Sarsden in their secluded retreats, and even the magnificent wool-church at Chipping Norton can be overlooked by the casual visitor to the town. But, when the western sun warms the honey-coloured stonework, Churchill church, so aptly named, re-states in its rural setting all the grace of Magdalen College tower at Oxford. It is a surprise, therefore, to discover that the church on its present site is a product of the nineteenth century revival of English Gothic architecture; the earlier church, which for many centuries was the spiritual centre of the village, stood in what is still the parish graveyard further down the hill, although there is little left to remind us of its former splendour.

The parish of Churchill is a coherent geographical area, shaped like a blunt wedge three miles long by one mile wide; it is contained between three water-courses: the River Evenlode in the south-west, and two of its small tributaries that separate Churchill from Kingham to the north-west (the Swail Brook), and from Sarsden to the south-east (the Sars Brook). On the north-east, the parish boundary follows the line of the 'Old London Road', thereby giving credence to the antiquity of this highway, before cutting across the fields to Meads Farm, to rejoin the stream half a mile above Swailsford Bridge. The parish of Sarsden, now so closely associated with Churchill, runs parallel to the south-east, although it is much narrower. In 1988, Della Hooke suggested that 'boundaries seem to have been drawn up deliberately to include all three types of land ... valley land suitable for cattle; arable on the better-drained soils where they were not too steep; and open downland, particularly suitable for sheep, with … occasional woodland'.[1] Churchill and Sarsden fit this description admirably.

The rocks underlying Churchill and Sarsden were deposited as sediments in the Lower and Middle Jurassic periods. One of the Middle Jurassic formations, the Chipping Norton Limestone that was laid down some 170 million years ago has yielded the fossilised bones of fishes, dinosaurs and pterosaurs (or flying reptiles) from old quarries to the north-east of Sarsden. The dinosaur remains comprise mainly isolated teeth of a species of megalosaur, a bipedal carnivorous animal about thirty feet long. There are also one or two bones of a brontosaur-like dinosaur. The pterosaur bones are, again, broken and isolated, and they represent a long-tailed animal about the size of a pigeon. A fossilised cetiosaurus – the first to be identified – was found nearby in Chipping Norton.

Five thousand years ago, this neighbourhood was inhabited by people of the New Stone Age. A remarkable collection of flint artefacts found on the Sarsden Estate was assembled by Lord Ducie and presented to Bristol City Museum where it is now preserved. It includes well over one hundred flint arrowheads ranging from the leaf-shaped to beautifully finished examples of barbed-and-tanged arrowheads, and several hundred flint scrapers of every variety. Since flint is not a local stone, all these artefacts must have been brought from some distance away, and the fact that so many have been found in such a restricted locality suggests that these were not lost or casually discarded but may well have been the equipment of a settled community. The large number of arrowheads indicates that the main occupation was hunting in the forest rather than farming. Sadly, as there is no documentation in the Ducie collection to indicate whereabouts in Sarsden they were found, it is unlikely that they were all together rather than scattered over the surface of the fields. Two rather suspect 'cooking stones' (pot boilers) are labelled as having been found in a 'Pit dwelling' in the 'Brash Quarry`. If so, then perhaps Lord Ducie excavated (and destroyed) a rare Neolithic habitation site.

---

1    Quoted in John Blair: Anglo-Saxon Oxfordshire, 1994, p.125.

There are Bronze Age round barrows at Squire's Clump in Sarsden, and at Mount Farm and in Besbury Lane in Churchill. In nearby Lyneham there is a small univallate hill fort known as Knollbury. The Romans, too, were here, and a recent find of a stone coffin led to the discovery in the early 1980s of the remains of a Roman villa in Churchill Grounds Farm. A villa was a Romanised farm with a primary interest in agriculture, constructed and owned by one of the more wealthy residents. It does not necessarily imply the presence of a Roman from Italy. Other villas have been located at North Leigh and Wigginton. The main Romano-British settlements locally were in Chipping Norton and on Kingham Hill, where villages might have helped to supply the labour needed on the villa estate[2].

---

2   See Martin Henig & Paul Booth, *Roman Oxfordshire*, 2000, pp 79ff.

# THE COMING OF THE CHRISTIAN FAITH

Angles and Saxons began to penetrate the South Midlands during the fifth century, and most of our present villages began as farms cleared by Saxon settlers. In this area, the settlers belonged to the northern fringe of the Hwicce tribe (hence 'Wychwood`) whose territory stretched from the Cotswolds to the Severn.[3] It is possible that the Hwicce absorbed a large element of the former Romano-British population of the area, amongst whom Christianity already existed; if so, they would have offered a fertile field for seventh century evangelism. The Christian message was brought to the region by an Irish missionary, Diuma, who as a young man had left his home to join St Aidan on Iona, and had travelled with him in 635 A.D. to establish the mission base on Lindisfarne whence wandering evangelists penetrated the Kingdom of Northumbria. Eighteen years later, a marriage alliance between Northumbria and Mercia enabled a Christian mission to accompany the royal bride to the heathen Midlands, and Diuma was consecrated bishop of the Middle Angles with his base at Lichfield. Despite the murder of his royal patron, Diuma continued his preaching missions, reaching the Cotswolds in 658 where apparently he met with great success. The Hwicce chief, Eanhere, became a Christian, thereby committing his tribe of seven thousand households to the new faith. Diuma, who by now was an old man, continued to evangelise on foot, penetrating the 'country called Infeppingham' which may have been the Forest of Wychwood. There he died, traditionally at Charlbury, on 7th December 658.

At first, the new faith was loosely structured on a network of monastic mission stations, cells of two or three monks that formed the 'old

---

3    See John Blair 'Anglo Saxon Oxfordshire', 1994, p.37, passim.

minsters' of which there may have been one at Daylesford or Evenlode. But the Upper Thames basin soon came under the more highly-organized control of the Roman Christian mission based at Dorchester, started by Birinus, a bishop who came from Frankish Gaul in about 633, landed at Southampton, and worked north into the area of the Middle Thames. He baptised Cynegils, King of the West Saxons, in 635, and established his diocesan base at Dorchester, where he died in 650. The Forest of Wychwood ('Hwicce-wood`) lay in the frontier region between the West Saxons and the Middle Angles. For many years it lay within the area controlled by the Kingdom of Mercia and it was not until later in the eighth century that it became clearly part of the Kingdom of Wessex and the Diocese of Dorchester[4]. The baptism of a king or chief would normally be followed by the baptism of all his followers, so that whole communities became nominally Christian at the same time.

By the ninth century, many villages would have had their own church building, even if this was an unpretentious structure of wood and thatch. The disturbances caused by the Viking invasions were a temporary setback to church growth – Dorchester had no bishop between 896 and 909 – but peace and prosperity in Wessex enabled church life to be restored in the eleventh century, and we can reasonably assume that there would have been a Saxon church in Churchill, as there was also in most other villages. Folk Paganism, however, died hard, as witnessed by the presence of a Holy Well on Kingham Hill within sight of Churchill church.

The Norman Conquest of 1066 imposed a new military and social ruling class of Norman barons and knights. Domesday Book (1086) says that Churchill was held by Walter de Vernon, but as his other lands lay in Cheshire it is likely that he installed a deputy in Churchill. Domesday records that Earl Harold of Wessex (King Harold) had held Churchill before 1066. The village included twenty-four villein[5] and fourteen

---

4    Blair, op. cit. p 56.

5    In feudal times, a member of a class of serfs who held the legal status of freemen in their dealings with all persons except their lord, to whom they owed certain services or rents in return for their land.

bordar[6] families, giving a population of over two hundred. The total area available for cultivation exceeded two thousand acres, but much of this was as yet undeveloped, as there were only twelve plough teams for land capable of employing twenty. There were also one hundred and seventy acres of meadow near the streams and one hundred and twenty acres of rough grazing, mostly in the upland area away from the village centre. The two water-mills valued at twenty shillings were probably situated at the foot of Hastings Hill and near Standbow Bridge on the River Evenlode where the adjacent field was later significantly called Milham.

The resident Norman knight was probably Henry de Chaldri, who held the land from Walter de Vernon on condition that he supplied Walter with a specified number of fighting men when required to do so. A Norman knight was expected to rebuild his parish church in stone in the Norman style, and then had the right to choose a priest or rector and present him to the bishop who would confirm him in the appointment before he could be installed. Bishop Remi had transferred his diocesan centre from Dorchester to Lincoln in 1072/3, as part of a general restructuring of the church. Churchill parish thereafter formed part of the Archdeaconry of Oxford in the enormous diocese of Lincoln until Henry VIII created five new dioceses (including Oxford) in 1542.

Some of the earliest records of the church at Churchill are preserved in the Cartulary of St Frideswide, and, as translated by the Revd Edmund Johnson, were printed by Mrs L.E.Rose in her *History of Churchill* (1934). Henry de Chaldri's daughter, Juliana, had married Henry de Noers, another Norman knight from Calvados, and had inherited Churchill thus bringing the manor into the hands of the de Noers (Nowers) family where it would remain until the end of the fifteenth century. In the earliest charter, dated to 1170-1180, Henry de Noers with the consent of his wife Juliana gave to the Priory of St Frideswide in Oxford the advowson or right to present a new rector for Churchill when a vacancy might occur, together with an endowment of the tithe payable

---

6    A tenant under the feudal system who held a small holding in return for menial services.

# DOMESDAY BOOK

*LIBER DE WINTONIA*

Compiled by direction of

## KING WILLIAM I

Winchester
1086

## LAND OF RICHARD OF COURCY

Idē.R.ten.xx.hid in *SECENDENE*.Tra.xxviii.car.
Nc̄ in dnīo.ix.car.7 xxx.iiii.ſerui.7 xxxvii.uilti cū.xxvi.
bord hñt.xix.car.Ibi.iii.molini de.xii.fot.7 clv.ac̄ p̄ti.
Paſtura.iiii.q̄rent lḡ.7 totid lat.Silua.i.leu lḡ.7 vii.q̄z lat.
T.R.E.ualb.xviii.lib.7 poſt 7 modo.xxvi.lib.    ⨍ 7 ual.x.ſot.
Idē.R.ten.i.hid in *FOXCOTE*.Tra.i.car.lbi.iiii.ac̄ p̄ti.Valuit

2  Richard also holds 20 hides in SARSDEN. Land for 28 ploughs.
Now in lordship 9 ploughs; 34 slaves.
    37 villagers with 26 smallholders have 19 ploughs.
    3 mills at 12s; meadow, 155 acres; pasture 4 furlongs long and
        as many wide; woodland 1 league long and 7 furlongs wide.
Value before 1066 £18; later and now £26.

3  Richard also holds 1 hide in FOSCOT. Land for 1 plough.
    Meadow, 4 acres.
The value is and was 10s.

## LAND OF EARL HUGH

Walteri ten de Comite *CERCELLE*.Ibi ſt.xx.hidæ.Tra
xx.car.Nc̄ in dnīo.iii.car.7 xxiiii.uilti cū.xiiii.bord hñt
ix.car.Ibi.ii.molini.xx.ſot.7 clxx.ac̄ p̄ti.7 cxx.ac̄ paſturæ.
Valuit 7 ual.x.lib.Herald tenuit.

Walter holds CHURCHILL from the Earl. 20 hides. Land for 20 ploughs.
Now in lordship 3 ploughs.
    24 villagers with 14 smallholders have 9 ploughs.
    2 mills, 20s; meadow, 170 acres; pasture, 120 acres.
The value is and was £10.  Earl Harold held it.

*Domesday Book entry*

on all his meadows. In return, of course, the Priory undertook to pray for the souls of Henry and Juliana de Noers in perpetuity. The Priory was entitled, if it wished, to become the corporate Rector of Churchill, thereby making the greater tithes directly payable to themselves, and to appoint a substitute or vicar to perform the priest's duties in the parish, but there is no evidence that they did so until the fourteenth century.

The charter from Henry and Juliana de Noers was one of many such gifts at that time, reflecting the general indignation felt at the murder of Archbishop Thomas Becket by four knights in Canterbury Cathedral on 29th December 1170, and its importance is attested by the need to have the charter confirmed in following years by Henry's son-in-law, Jordan; his son, Nicholas; his overlord, Richard Vernon; Richard de Nevers; Juliana's second husband, William de Mandeville; John de Constantis, Archdeacon of Oxford; Richard, Archbishop of Canterbury, and Pope Alexander III. One of these confirmations, dated about 1190, was witnessed by Stephen the Clerk (amongst others), who may have been the first-known Rector of Churchill.

Trouble with St Frideswide's began in about 1210 when Nicholas de Noers, son of Henry and Juliana, seems to have given a hide of land (about one hundred and twenty acres) in Churchill to the monks of Bruern Abbey, in return for a promise that he could be buried in the Abbey. Mrs Rose identified this land, probably correctly, as Grange Farm. The great tithes on this land were still payable to St Frideswide's, but the monks of Bruern Abbey withheld them, and took the tithes for themselves. The matter required the intervention of Pope Honorius III who in 1217 ordered that all the tithes must be paid to St Frideswide's Priory. The monks, however, were not so easily defeated, and in 1220 they secured an adjustment in their favour. Nicholas de Noers, no doubt in an attempt to appease the Canons of St Frideswide, made an additional grant to the Priory of a plot of land in Churchill 'which lies before the rector's gate`. This is the first documentary evidence for the existence of a rectory or parsonage house in Churchill. Presumably this was the same piece of land as the one described in detail in another charter of the same period (1220-1230) from Matthew le Sethne: it was only a very small piece of land – about thirty yards long and eighteen yards wide.

The contentious issue of tithes was taken up again in 1241 and 1253, this time by John, Rector of Churchill, who was, of course, the man personally affected by this matter. A mandate of Pope Gregory IX dated 1241 exempted the monks of Bruern Abbey from the payment of tithes of hay on one-and-a-half hides and one acre of land given by Nicholas de Nowers, but for the sake of peace they were required to pay the rector ten shillings annually.

Finally, on 2nd February 1253/4, it was decreed that 'the wall and enclosure given to the monks of Bruern by Nicholas de Nowers shall continue to be theirs, free from further lawsuit, on condition that they might have the whole of the common land of Churchill as their pasture land as far as the Evenlode and back, for the purpose of watering and feeding, whenever the Evenlode meadows are flooded, mown, and the hay is being carried, as was the custom in the old days before the aforementioned John lived`. One can deduce from these documents that the monks of Bruern had won their long battle over tithes, which were now commuted for a small annual payment, and this settlement was ratified by the agreement of all the freemen of Churchill (whose rights on the common pasture land were affected) in 1254. The eighteen named freemen were the owners of land in Churchill, in addition to the land held by the lord of the manor.

# THE MEDIEVAL CHURCH

The medieval church was situated near what is now called Hastings Hill, and the old village of Churchill was behind and below it. In a dry summer, the outlines of the foundations of the old cottages can still be clearly seen in the pasture field behind the churchyard. There was certainly a building there by 1170, which was probably reconstructed and extended later. The tenuous architectural evidence from a nineteenth century engraving, supported by recent archaeological investigation, suggests that Churchill church was reconstructed in the early fourteenth century in the Decorated style. It is impossible now to determine whether this was undertaken by Sir Roger de Nowers before 1336 in order to assert his prerogative as patron and to emulate the rebuilding of Kingham church by his rival, Ralph de Chasteleyn, or whether it was undertaken by St Frideswide's in the 1340s. In any case, it is likely to have been completed before 1348/9 when the Black Death dramatically reduced the population, thus limiting the available labour force and removing the pressure for increased accommodation in the church.

The old church must have been sizable. It consisted of chancel, central tower, nave, south aisle and south porch and its outlines can still be discerned in the churchyard. It is believed that the original chancel arch has survived as the west doorway of the present Heritage Centre; if so, it was very small for a chancel arch, and it seems more likely that this was the original south doorway moved into its new position during the restoration of 1869. From a drawing made of the church during its demolition in 1826, it seems possible that a new extension was made to the twelfth century church in the early fourteenth century, since the east window in the chancel and the windows in the south aisle appear to belong to the Decorated style of architecture.

*All Saints Church 1801*

In the Domesday Book of 1086, the manor of Sarsden appears to have had the largest population of any village in north-west Oxfordshire. Allowing for unintentional underestimates, the population of Sarsden seems to have been at least five hundred and fifty, with a surprisingly large proportion of serfs (slaves). By comparison, Hook Norton, the second largest manor in the district, had a population of about four hundred and seventy, and [Chipping] Norton of about three hundred. Sarsden was therefore more than twice as large as Churchill (with about two hundred and twenty inhabitants). The extensive acreage of Sarsden included a broad belt of forest land, one league wide, for Sarsden lay within the boundaries of the Forest of Wychwood, and Richard de Courcy, Lord of Sarsden, also owned the tiny hamlet of Foscote on the west bank of the River Evenlode. During the thirteenth century much of the Wychwood area was afforested, although this was a technicality to enable the land to be hunted and to be subject to the Forest Laws. It may not necessarily have been wooded.

It is probably too simple to explain the decline of Sarsden solely as a result of the Black Death (1348-9). But by the middle of the fourteenth century, Sarsden churchyard had fallen into disuse and seems to have been officially closed by ecclesiastical order. Thereafter, the burials of Sarsden parishioners all took place in Churchill. At a burial, the officiating rector or vicar was entitled to claim a mortuary fee from the estate of the deceased. In theory this was his second-best chattel, or its financial equivalent, and was supposed to represent tithes that he had forgotten to pay. Mortuary fees – the origin of today's burial fees – were always unpopular, but they represented a considerable element in the vicar's stipend or salary. When the Sarsden churchyard was closed, the Rector of Sarsden lost his right to claim mortuary fees that were now all payable to the Vicar of Churchill.

This led to increasing ill-feeling between the Rector of Sarsden and the Vicar of Churchill, and in 1375 the vicar accused Philip Montgomery, Rector of Sarsden, of withholding the mortuary fees from his parishioners. Judgment in favour of Churchill was given on 6th November 1375:

> And let it be remembered that Churchill Church from long ago was accustomed to have the mortuary fees of all and singular the parishioners of the village of Sarsden, dying there, whose corpses have their last farewell and grave at Churchill, whence the aforesaid [Churchill] church has a certain portion in the village [of Sarsden], namely that they receive annually from the lord of the same village of Sarsden two acres of corn, one of wheat and the other of oats, and the third part of eggs.

By agreement of the Rector of Sarsden, these fees were commuted into an annual money payment of six shillings and eight pence (half a mark or 33p in modern terms, but of course far more valuable then), with a further half-mark for arrears. Until the eighteenth century, calculations were usually made in multiples of marks, even though no such coin was ever minted. It is interesting that, as late as 1827, parishioners of Sarsden still asserted their separate status and retained their own burial register even though no burials had taken place in Sarsden for nearly five hundred years.

The village of Sarsden never recovered its earlier size and significance. The great house – Sarsden House – survived, with the adjoining parish church that became almost the private chapel of the Lord of the Manor. A small group of cottages constituted the village, and there was a scatter of outlying homesteads. But the remains of the Village Cross still stand as a reminder that Sarsden had once been more significant.

*St James Church Sarsden*

The procedure for paying the vicar his stipend proved unsatisfactory to all concerned. Tithes, gifts and fees from the parish were remitted to the Priory of St Frideswide's in Oxford who paid the vicar his stipend only once every two years. The vicar was obliged to cultivate his glebe land, which he held by virtue of his office, as his own smallholding. This state of affairs continued until 1398 when the vicar, William Grom, and the Prior and Canons of St Frideswide applied to Henry Beaufort, Bishop of Lincoln, to regulate the payment of the stipend:

*It has been notified to us that our vicarage of the afore-mentioned parish church [of Churchill] is supported by a certain sum of* money that the Convent [St Frideswide's] pays to the vicar once in two years; that it would be more convenient to the vicar and his successors (as it seems to him for many reasons frankly told us then by the Vicar himself) that the endowment should be derived from the tithes and gifts and other offerings which come in at odd times to the parish church aforesaid. He asks that we make a new endowment by means of first fruits. Brother Thomas Bradwell, the Prior of the Priory of St Frideswide aforesaid, asserts on behalf of himself and the convent that it has been and is now a serious and burdensome matter for himself and for the Priory to collect the great and small tithes and gifts and other offerings to the aforesaid church which is more than twenty miles away from Oxford and then obtain money for their equivalent and to make an annual payment to the vicar as they have described. We have been asked in a humble and obedient manner, in the same way and for the same thing that the vicar asked, that we should graciously condescend to come to the relief of the Prior in this matter.

So, being influenced by many other reasons that we should do this with the consent of each party, we now order expressly that the aforementioned Vicar of the Parish Church of Churchill, whoever he might be, shall receive as long as he holds the living, from the parish church aforesaid, in the name of the vicar of that church, all gifts which the whole of the parish pay him four times a year beginning with February 2nd, shall be made to him, and also the fees arising from marriage, churchings, and funerals, also from the parishioners of Sarsden, and for Saints' Days; also for the monuments erected in the said church of whatever kind and wherever they may be placed. The payments shall be brought, by right and custom and willingly, in the form of wax or money, sheep or grain, and the fourth part of the fees of funerals that may occur of the said parishioners who are buried away from Churchill as being rightly not the custom of the parish church.

That the vicar shall receive all the tithes of calves, lambs, chickens, pigs, rabbits, hawks, eggs, and also from the parishioners of

Sarsden he shall receive the tithes of milk, linen, hemp, all kinds of fruit (such as apples and pears) of honey and of fruits of every kind from the time of its growth and when it is brought to the miller at Churchill.

Also he will receive the tithes of all the odds and ends of skins which otherwise would not be paid in money. Also all the tithes that come from game, fish, merchandise, smith's work, and from bartering of whatsoever description.

Also all the matters connected with death (to include the parishioners of Sarsden) alive or dead unless a bona fide payment be made of some kind for the burial rite, such as a horse or an ox.

The aforesaid vicar shall have, and his successors shall have, just such a residence which the present man has, suitable and commanding respect for his office, and the outside buildings to be of a like description. The convent shall make provision for this.

Also the vicar now holds what his predecessors had, namely ten acres of arable land, as follows: five acres of land in one field and five acres in the other, with a meadow adjoining each in proportion. It is admitted that he now has these ten acres with the meadow.

And in the future the Vicar of Churchill shall pay the fees connected with the Archdeacon's Visitation for the time when they are due and also he will bear the responsibility, which before the convent did, of providing candles, incense, bread and wine for the aforesaid church. All other outgoing the convent will bear and account for.

We make this present regulation by the expressed consent of the aforesaid religious men [Prior and Canons] and the vicar, as it has been submitted, reserving to ourselves from this document and to our successors the power of changing, correcting, adding, taking away and making clear should there be any loss or error or doubt arising from dishonesty.

The vicar has a respectable parsonage house (the term 'vicarage' refers to his office and not his residence) and ten strips or ridges of arable land scattered between the two great Open Fields. These acres were each probably twenty-two yards wide and two hundred and twenty yards (a furlong) long, and were cultivated in the same way as the custom was for the rest of the village. The 'churching of women' (a service still preserved in the 1662 Prayer Book) was the thanksgiving of a mother after childbirth; she traditionally wore a white veil, sat in a specially designated place in church, and made a thankoffering to the vicar.

This rather pompous document incidentally throws light on the daily lives of the villagers – their bees, rabbits, apples and pears, fish caught in the stream, oxen, horses, cows for milk, calves and lambs, linen and hemp for weaving, skins for tanning, hawks for hawking and wax for candles. It was not ungenerous, and the 'religious men' of St Frideswide's had made substantial concessions for the maintenance of the vicar.

# THE EARLY TUDOR PERIOD

Mrs Lilian Rose took considerable trouble to trace the lordship of the manor of Churchill from the time of its sale to John Drayton in 1447 until its partial acquisition in 1587[1583?] by Sir Christopher Hatton. The Barantyne (Barentine) family inherited the manor from John Drayton and retained it until the late sixteenth century. However, the Barantynes did not reside in Churchill, but in one of their other manors at Chalgrove or in the parish of Great Haseley. John Barentine of Haseley was briefly Sheriff of Oxfordshire in 1464-5. In his will (1474), he made substantial bequests to the Order of Friars Preachers (Dominicans or Blackfriars) who had a fraternal House in Oxford. After his death, his widow and teenage son were involved in lawsuits with the de Nowers family over the lordship of Churchill.

In the absence of the lord, the manor was administered by a resident bailiff who would have lived in the manor house. But by the seventeenth century the manor house was leased to wealthy tenants such as George Morecroft.

When Cardinal Wolsey suppressed St Frideswide's Priory in 1517 in order to create his own Cardinal College at Oxford, the advowson of Churchill was automatically transferred to the new institution. Churchill is omitted from the records of the Bishop of Lincoln's Visitation in 1517. In 1530, Cardinal College was listed as the patron of the living of Churchill, and the churchwardens, William Gowes and William Menchen, reported that 'all is well'. All things were not so well in Sarsden: in 1517 the Sarsden churchwardens reported that the seats (sedilia – seats for the clergy) in the church were ruined and the rector had nowhere to live. In 1530 Sarsden Church was still not fully repaired, although they *are getting round to repairing it'*.

Following the fall of Cardinal Wolsey, Henry VIII visited Oxford in 1532, and transferred Cardinal College into his own name. Twelve years later, it was re-named Christ Church and the former chapel of St Frideswide's Priory became Oxford Cathedral. The advowson – the right to present a vicar for Churchill – passed to the crown (who exercised the right in 1554, 1557 and 1581) but apparently sold it into private ownership.

One of the more colourful Barentine lords was Sir William Barentine (1481-1549). A disadvantage of having a non-resident Lord of the Manor – for there is no evidence that Sir William ever set foot in Churchill – was that there was no longer a personal interest in the village, and the lord was unacquainted with his tenants there. For Sir William Barentine who inherited the manor in 1484, (aged five), this meant that he could speculate in land purchases, and could treat his manor of Churchill as his private estate although by manorial custom the villagers – 'copyholders' – also should have had their own rights. In early Tudor times, there was extensive private enclosure of arable land for the more profitable sheep farming. These enclosures were bitterly unpopular as they inevitably led to the eviction of peasants and to depopulation, and Cardinal Wolsey took active steps to check the spread of this new development. Churchill probably suffered more severely than any other village in Oxfordshire: Wolsey's Enclosure Commission of 1517 reported that on 16th October 1512, Sir William Barentine had enclosed three hundred acres of arable land in Churchill. Land that had formerly been cultivated under the old open field system, was enclosed by hedges for sheep to graze. One shepherd could do the work of many peasants, and the wealth of the Barentines was founded in wool. About sixteen cottages in the village were abandoned, and their occupants had to seek work elsewhere, perhaps as labourers rather than as peasants. The Enclosure Commissioners reported that Sir William's speculation was paying dividends: the rental value of the manor of Churchill had risen from £15 to £41 per annum.

Sir William Barentine was an influential man. He was Sheriff of Oxfordshire three times, and was knighted by Henry VIII in 1513 at Tournai where he commanded his own 'retinue' of twenty-two men.. He also owned and commanded his own ship of one hundred tons –

the 'Trinity Dytton' – with a very large crew of two hundred and fifty-nine men, which he placed at the king's service when duty required although it seems he was not averse to a spot of piracy against the French in the Channel from time to time. In 1516 he was a Justice of the Peace for the City of Oxford and from 1524 to 1548 he was also a Justice for Oxfordshire. He was in the king's army in France in 1520, and again in 1522. In 1543 he was one of the eight Oxfordshire 'notables' who commanded the county's contingent of two hundred men to help defend the Low Countries against the French: Sir William's contribution was twenty footmen. He was an M.P. in 1529 and probably again in 1536. In 1529 he wrote to his 'heartily beloved friend, Master Cromwell'[7] inviting him to visit the Barentine mansion at Haseley Court, and incidentally asking to be allowed to farm (that is, to administer) the land of Churchill Parsonage. Once the Papal supremacy had been overthrown, he took an active role in the affairs of the new regime, even though his own religious sympathies seem to have been with the Catholic position. He served on the commission in 1539 to enforce the royal supremacy over the church, and was later one of the commissioners who sentenced the Abbot of Reading to death for daring to deny Henry VIII's newly assumed powers. When the monasteries were dissolved during the years 1536-40, he speculated in buying former monastic lands from the Court of Augmentations, and then reselling them at a profit. Mrs Rose says (page 62) that in his will *he stated that he had bought Churchill Farm from Sir Thomas Pope. It is called elsewhere Churchill Grange and is undoubtedly the Grange Farm that is there now and was the estate mentioned in the old charters as belonging to Bruern Monastery.* Bruern Abbey was one of those that were dissolved in 1536, and was then sold to Thomas Pope. In 'The Lords Lieutenants and High Sheriffs of Oxfordshire'[8] the author says that *the importance of [his] estate in Churchill is further suggested by his acquisition in 1544 of the manorial rights, which had previously belonged to Bruern Abbey.* Since there is no suggestion elsewhere that the Barentines had ever surrendered the manorial rights of Churchill, this must surely be a misinterpretation of the purchase of Churchill Grange (Farm) from Thomas Pope. Mrs Joy

---

7    Thomas Cromwell, Henry VIII's Secretary

8    Christine Peters, 1995, page 77

Timms, who has thoroughly researched the records of Bruern Abbey and for whose help I am particularly grateful, strongly concurs with this interpretation.

Sir William married three times, and had eight children in all. His second marriage to Jane Lewknor was challenged in Chancery on the grounds that Jane had taken a vow of perpetual chastity at the death of her previous husband in 1536. This cast doubt on the legitimacy of Sir William's son and heir, Francis, and, although Chancery decided that the vow of chastity was invalid since it had been obtained by extortion, the Lewknors and Barentines were still engaged in litigation in 1563. Sir William Barentine died on 17th November 1549 and was buried in the Old Church at Churchill. Anthony Wood[9] said that over the belfry door in the church were displayed the arms of Barentine, Drayton and Popham. He was succeeded by his son, Francis Barentine, who died in 1557.

When in 1543 Henry VIII mustered an army from all able-bodied men between the ages of sixteen and sixty, seven men were selected in Churchill: William Salcome, Thomas Salcome and Thomas Irton were three tall strong men capable of drawing a longbow; William Sessions, Rauf Atherton, William Collys and Symond Whiting were drawn as billmen, each carrying a pike with a hook or a blade fixed to the business end, and in addition 'the Towne' (that is, the village) had to produce a further archer and billman in armour.[10]

---

9   (1632-1695) was an Oxford antiquary. His History of Oxford, Athenae Oxonienses, notebooks and Autobiography contain many valuable, curious and recondite pieces of information relating to the city and county.

10  *The Oxfordshire Muster Rolls*, ed Peter Beauchamp, ORS Vol 60, 1996. Peter Beauchamp is descended from the local family by that name.

# TWO ELIZABETHAN VICARS

Many changes in parish life took place during the Reformation period (c.1517-1562). An indication of the disturbed times came in 1554 when the Bishop of Oxford, a diocese newly-created in 1542, denied Humphrey Huntpack institution as Vicar of Churchill. Huntpack had been presented by the Catholic Queen Mary I. In his place, Humphrey Bowyer (Boyer) was instituted vicar on 29th January 1555/6 and stayed for twenty-four years, conforming to the establishment of the Anglican Church by the Elizabethan settlement of religion, and using the English Prayer Book of 1562. There is evidence, however, that Humphrey Bowyer like many of his fellow priests may secretly have hoped for a return to the traditional Catholic rites and usage, for he seems illegally to have preserved the parish vestments and relics, that had already survived the drastic changes during the reign of Edward VI, and on his deathbed entrusted them to Henry Medcroft who was probably churchwarden. Humphrey Bowyer retired in 1581 but continued to live in Churchill until his death two years later. His will, proved on 4th April 1583, gives a glimpse into the simple lifestyle of a celibate sixteenth century parish priest, who still probably farmed his own glebe land.

*Item: I geve and bequeathe to Raphe Webster all my workinge daies apparrell, that is to saie, a coate, a dublet, a shirt, a paire of hoses, a paire of shoes and a capp. Item: I geve unto Jone Carter my blewe gowne. Item: I geve unto Anne Carter xii d. Item: I geve unto Edward Carter one blacke gowne and my olde letheron dublet. Item: I geve unto Elizabethe Budd and Katheren Waters ether of them ii d and to old Mother Hope ii d. Item: I geve unto Raphe Webster his wife and everie one of her residue ii d a peece. Item: I will that ii dozen of Bread be geven amonge the poore at the daie of my buriall. Item: I geve unto everie scholler that is at my buriall a pennie. Item: I geve unto everie one in the almes house of Norton (beinge aged) a pennie...*

It is surprising to notice that there appears to have been a small school in Churchill as early as 1583, whose scholars no doubt packed the funeral in order to claim their penny.

Richard Baguley (Bagley), who became Vicar of Churchill in 1581, found himself in serious trouble in the Archdeacon's Court three years later. On 31st March 1584, enquiries in the village brought to light rumours of immorality between the vicar and Emma Nash of Churchill. Each week during July and August that year, Richard Baguley and Emma Nash were summoned to appear in the Archdeacon's Court to face these charges. In her defence, Emma Nash denied 'that ever he had to doe with her neither that he did attempt the same, but saith that upon occasion goinge for some salve at master vicar's request she was searched by divers honest women of Churchill whether she had burned him or not; and whether she was sound'. The vicar was required to clear himself by compurgation – the oaths of three neighbouring clergy – which he appears to have obtained. But Emma Nash was less fortunate: failing to obtain the compurgation of four neighbours, she was excommunicated, and Richard Baguley was required to see the sentence carried out. This all sounds as though it could have been malicious village gossip, but the churchwardens had taken it seriously enough to report it to the archdeacon.

The archdeacon, however, had not finished with Richard Baguley. While investigating the rumours of immorality, he discovered that Baguley did not always wear the surplice. There had been prolonged national controversy over the restoration of ecclesiastical vestments in 1559, but Archbishop Parker's 'Advertisements' of 1566 required the use of a linen surplice (but no other vestments) in church as part of the official clothing of the clergy at divine service and at the sacraments. Richard Baguley stated 'that he doeth sumetymes in divine service use his surples and weare yt and sumetymes useth it not'. This suggests that he shared some of the prejudices of the Elizabethan Puritans. He was told that he must wear a surplice during divine service. A further charge brought on 13th February 1584/5 was that he was guilty of pluralism. Baguley admitted that he had served the cure of the parish of Sarsden together with 'the Churchill cure bye the space of ii yeares', and was told that he must no longer serve anywhere except in his own parish. His real offence, of course, was in omitting to obtain – and pay for – the necessary dispensation.

Shaw, the archdeacon's apparitor or summoner, whose duty was to ensure the attendance at the Archdeacon's Court of those people who had been summoned for ecclesiastical offences, did his job thoroughly. Not satisfied with the exposure of the vicar, he had also located some of the hidden vestments and furnishings of the pre-Reformation church. In 1552-3, the government of Edward VI had ordered the confiscation of all the valuable church plate and furnishings except for one chalice and the church bells; but there is no record of any confiscation taking place either in Churchill or Sarsden. On 6[th] March 1584/5, William Lucas of Churchill, who was presumably a churchwarden, was summoned for 'kepinge of coopes [copes] etc.' In reply he said that 'he knoweth not wheare there chalice is become or in whose custodie it remayneth nether doth he know of any other relicques of superstic[i]on to remayne in anye man's handes within there parishe, and saith further that he receyved the parcells exhibited and also so mutche as he sould for xvi s of one Henry Medcroste [Medcrofte] and William Minchen of the said parish.' William Minchen and Henry Medcrofte were next summoned for keeping relics. Presumably they were former churchwardens, and William Minchen was certainly old enough to have a personal knowledge of what had happened at the time of the Edwardian Reformation. Being questioned as to his age, he said that he was aged sixty-one or more years, and was a native of Churchill parish. He had 'receyvid one of the said relickes exhibited of Mr Boyer, there late vicar, at the time of his death', and added that he and Henry Medcrofte 'did deliver a crosse of brasse to the bellfounder to make a saunce bell withal'. Presumably this was the sanctus or sacring bell used during the communion service. Lastly, Henry Medcrofte was summoned for 'deleying of relicques', and he confessed 'that there was about a vi or vii yeares agoe in the custodie of one William Kerrie three copes or vestmentes, one of velvit and ii of silke and too crosses, of which they tooke one of the crosses and put it to the belfounders in Oxford to make their sauncebell withal, which said relicques have remained in the custodie of this respondent ever since undefaced until they by chaunce came to light of late'. Henry Medcrofte was sentenced to do a penance for his part in this innocuous deception. One can deduce that Humphrey Bowyer, who had been appointed vicar in the Counter-Reformation period of Mary I, was sympathetic to the old religion, and, finding the medieval vestments and furnishings still in existence, had decided to preserve them in the hope that times would change again. Perhaps the churchwardens had more mercenary motives for wishing to hold on to their parish assets.

Summoner Shaw had been really active during his visit to Churchill, or else he had encountered a sixteenth century super-grass there. He also discovered that two women, Anne Carpenter and Anne Hall, had given birth to illegitimate children, and they also were brought before the Archdeacon's Court, found guilty, and sentenced to do penance. There is no reference to what, if anything, happened to the fathers of the children. One wonders whether life in Churchill was always as exciting as it appears to have been in the year for which the proceedings of the Archdeacon's Court are available.[11]

Richard Baguley remained Vicar of Churchill until 1601, when he died intestate. Administration of his property was granted on 8th October to his widow, Anne Baguley, and amounted to the modest sum of £18 – 3s – 10d. Presumably he was the first married Vicar of Churchill.

The heir of the Barentines – Sir Walter Harcourt of Stanton Harcourt – sold the manor of Churchill to Sir Christopher Hatton in 1583. Sir Christopher Hatton (c.1540 – 1591) was another colourful but non-resident lord of the manor. His biographer, Eric St John Brooks, himself a descendant of the Brooks family of Churchill, ('Sir Christopher Hatton', Oxford, 1946) wrote little about the tenuous Churchill connection. On one occasion, Hatton's secretary, Samuel Cox, wrote on his behalf to Dr William James, the Rector of Kingham, requiring that he should enforce the legally binding betrothal of the miller of Kingham to a girl

---

11 'The Archdeacon's Court`, ORS Vol XXIII, 1942

from Churchill. Dr James wrote a sensible but compassionate reply, agreeing that, although the marriage could be enforced, the miller was so resolutely opposed to it that little pleasure or benefit would result from such a marriage. Unfortunately we do not know what the outcome of this correspondence was.

Sir Christopher Hatton, although of humble origins, rose to prominence as one of the bachelor favourites of Queen Elizabeth I, 'being young and of a comely tallness of body and amiable countenance'. He was a tilter or jouster for the Queen's amusement in 1561 and 1571. The Queen then began to load him with honours and offices: he became a Gentleman of the Queen's Privy Council, Captain of the Queen's Bodyguard (the Yeomen of the Guard), Receiver of Tenths and First Fruits (a tax on the clergy) in 1578 and in 1587 was given the Order of the Garter and made Chancellor of Oxford University and Lord Chancellor of England. He also had the engaging pastime of collecting the large wax seals appended in place of signatures to official documents; in consequence historians now have an excellent collection of unusual documents to which the seals had once been attached. It was generally believed that the Queen's favour arose more from his accomplishments as a dancer than for his genuine skill as a lawyer, but this underestimates his considerable legal and political ability.

As Sir Christopher never married, he made elaborate provision for the inheritance of his estates after his death. He died on 20th November 1591, and his immediate heir was his nephew and adopted son, William Hatton (Newport). When Sir William died, the next heir was Hatton's second cousin, Christopher Hatton of Stanton, Cambridgeshire, aged sixteen, but, before he could inherit, the government instituted an enquiry into Sir Christopher's misappropriation of funds by virtue of his office as Receiver of Tenths and First Fruits. The total debt amounted to about £42,000 – a prodigious sum in those days – in accordance with which the Hatton estates were 'extended' – forfeited to the crown – and young Christopher Hatton became a ward of the crown. The estates in Churchill were subject to two inquisitions in 1597. Finally, by Act of Parliament in 1605, young Christopher Hatton was permitted to inherit the Hatton estates, and to sell them, on condition that he repaid

Sir Christopher's debt at the rate of £1,500 a year. He sold the manor of Churchill to Francis Dormer, although there seems still to have been some uncertainty as in 1629 the estates were said to be in the hands of the 'heirs of Sir Christopher Hatton'. It later appears to have been acquired by George Morecroft, eldest son of the Rector of Kingham.

Mrs Lilian Rose is probably correct in thinking that Christopher Hatton sold off his land in Churchill piecemeal, and prosperous yeoman families in the village – Hackers, Brooks, Sessions, Jetts and Mullingtons – were able to buy their own property.

# A TIME OF TROUBLES

By contrast with the neighbouring Churchill, Sarsden began to regain influence in the seventeenth century. The Lordship of the Manor of Sarsden passed into the hands of the Walter family, who also later became Lords of the Manor of Churchill. Sir John Walter was Chief Baron of the Exchequer. His younger son, David Walter, purchased the manor of Wolvercote, including the Wolvercote Mills (fulling mill and corn mill) in Oxford in 1616, and was buried at Wolvercourt in 1679, at which time his elder brother, Sir William Walter of Sarsden, inherited the manor of

*Sir John Walter of Sarsden (1673-1722)*

Wolvercote. In about 1627 Sir John Walter took pity on the poverty of the vicar of Churchill whose stipend was valued at no more than £14 a year. Sir John augmented this stipend with a gift of £50 p.a. 'for the perpetual maintenance of a Preacher at Churchill`, and confirmed this in his will where he secured the payment by the rents from a grant of land at Merriscourt and elsewhere. This endowment at Churchill created what was then known as a Lectureship for the parish, which was often a Puritan ploy to guarantee a scriptural teaching ministry at a time when Laudian High Church clergy were in the ascendant. Sir John made a similar grant of £50 to 'increase the living of the parson at Sarsden', which suggests that the advowson of both parishes was now held by the Lords of the Manor of Sarsden. Sir John died in 1630 and was succeeded by his son, Sir William Walter. Sir William Walter had been born c.1603, educated at Christ Church, Oxford, and became a lawyer. He was M.P. for Weobley in 1628, and High Sheriff of Oxfordshire in 1636. In 1641 he was created a baronet by King Charles I, and took an active part in supporting the royalists during the early part of the Civil War.

Several interesting memorial inscriptions in the old church belong to this period, and were recorded by Dr A Hutton in his 'Oxfordshire Monumental Inscriptions'. The best-known of these, which may still be seen, is the delightful epitaph in verse to John Gostwick, Gent., who died aged 75 on 10th February 1618/9. This was on a brass plate fixed to a plain white stone under the Communion Table, but was subsequently re-fixed to the east wall of the old chancel:

*Stay gentle reader yf thou dost enquire*
*Who Mr Gostwick was Have thy desire.*
*A Gentleman he was, of antient name*
*And welbelov'd of all that to him came.*
*At th'University and then att Court*
*He had his times of study and resort.*
*After all this he toke delight to dwell*
*Att his devotions in his private cell.*
*Happy old man w'ch so his youth could spend*
*That he was happy att his latter end.*

Although the parish registers of Sarsden date from 1576, those of Churchill have survived from only 1630, and omit the period of civil registration during the Commonwealth regime.

On 27th September 1633, the churchwardens of Churchill, William Sessions and Thomas Shurley, brought a case in the church courts against George Moorecrofte [junior] and George Dodford the Elder, both well-to-do residents in the village, for refusing to contribute to two legal taxes raised in the parish for the repair of Churchill church. The repairs were estimated to cost £10 and included a new roof to the porch, repairs to the leads, the windows and the pavements (floors). It also needed 'a new surplice for the vicar, bell ropes and a great chest with locks and keys which ought to be in the church.' There were no set means or revenues belonging to the church from which to pay for repairs. They were paid for by the inhabitants of Churchill and others who held land there. The churchwardens had twice after morning prayer in church made a formal announcement of their intention to raise a tax that they had assessed at very moderate amounts according to the ability of individual parishioners to pay. There is no record of the outcome of this case, but with Bishop William Laud dominant both in church and state it is unlikely that the offenders escaped punishment. Even the Walters of Sarsden did not escape the churchwardens' criticism: '*About five or six years ago Lord [sic] Walter had allotted certain of his lands in Churchill for the Church and the poor but his heir had taken the benefit of most of them into his own hands and it was not available to the church or the poor.*`

Two members of the Glyn (Glynne) family were vicars of Churchill through much of the seventeenth century. Edmund Glyn was appointed vicar in 1601, and subscribed to the Protestation Oath in 1641/2. Very shortly after the burial of his wife, Ankerett (Ancarrett) on 25th June 1643, Edmund Glyn resigned the living and was succeeded by his son, Benjamin. Benjamin Glyn (1613-1697) is the only incumbent of Churchill known to have been born in the parish. He graduated at the recently founded Wadham College, Oxford, on 16th February 1636/7, and was ordained a few months later. When his father resigned, Benjamin was presented as Vicar of Churchill on 27th December 1643 by King Charles I who was then living in Christ Church, Oxford. It is not unreasonable to assume that Benjamin was an active royalist.

The Protestation Oath of 1641/2 arose from the political machinations in Parliament by John Pym against Charles I's government. Its avowed purpose was to prove the massive popular support throughout the country against 'all Popery and Popish Innovations`, by which he implied the undue influence of Thomas Wentworth, Earl of Strafford, the catholic Queen Henrietta Maria and the High Church Archbishop Laud. In the end its political significance was negligible, and it is chiefly important for us today in that the parish returns contain the names of all parishioners aged eighteen and over. Led by the parish priest, churchwardens, overseers of the poor and the village constable, the parishioners were required to take the oath and to sign their names or, as more often, to mark their name with a cross. The oaths were sworn in the presence of a Justice of the Peace, usually in a nearby market town, on various dates early in February 1641/2.

The Protestation from Churchill has survived where 'all have consented, none refused'. There are over one hundred names, and several were able to sign for themselves which suggests that a village school may still have been in existence. The Sarsden return, however, has not been preserved. Although the men listed were not all heads of households, it is possible to use the accepted multiplier of 3 to estimate the population of Churchill in 1642 as about 306. Of these, presumably the wealthiest can be identified from the Estreate for the Chadlington Hundred[12]. These were Augustus Skynner Esq., George Moorcroft Esq., Thomas Sessions, Giles Harris, John Whytley, William Bridge, Revd George Moorcroft (Rector of Kingham) assessed on lands, and Anne Hacker, widow, assessed in goods. The Estreate for Sarsden lists William Walter Esq., Mary Clapton, widow, Francis Haslewood, John Rawlyns and Robert Boys.

It is not likely that Churchill saw any actual fighting during the Civil Wars (1642-6, 1648-9), although the villagers will have been all too familiar with royalist cavalry from Oxford and parliamentary troopers from Compton Wynyates. Churchill lay in an area contested by both sides, with the king in his capital in the City of Oxford, and Parliament centred on its strongholds in Coventry and Gloucester. On 12th May 1643, the royalist garrison at Oxford received four muskets from Thomas Sessions, gentleman, of Churchill. In October 1643 the Roundhead army of the Earl of Essex marched from Chipping Norton to Stow on its way to raise the siege of Gloucester, and a year later King Charles I led his army from Deddington to Broadway by way of Chipping Norton and Moreton-in-Marsh. As the years passed, taxes and extortions levied by both sides made daily life intolerable. On 10th June 1644, Captain

---

12 1641, printed in M. Sturge Henderson, *'Three Centuries of North Oxfordshire'*, Oxford, 1902, pages 228-229).

Henry Stevens, Waggon-Master-General to the king, was desperately trying to find food for the garrison in Oxford. 'Whereas it is further informed that there are 500 quarters of Corne at Churchill, Chadlington and Saresden, he is also forthwith to take the like care for bringing in the same [to Oxford] where the Owner shall have like liberty to sell the same For the effecting whereof, the Governor is desired to assigne him Parties of Horse when he shall desire them'[13]. It is unlikely that the owner of the corn was ever recompensed. Sympathies in the villages were mixed: Churchill seems to have been mainly royalist whereas Kingham was parliamentarian, but most people probably hoped that the war would keep far away from their village. From 1646 to 1649, George Morecroft, the unrepentant royalist Rector of Kingham, took refuge with his son in Churchill; whence he launched two strong but unsuccessful attempts, by 'force and arms', to regain his parish and his parsonage. In 1650, Mistress Anne Hacker of Churchill, the widow of Thomas Hacker who died in 1638, was fined the exorbitant sum of £25 for lending a horse to the royalists, presumably during the Second Civil War of 1648. The Hackers were by this time the dominant yeoman family in Churchill, and Anne Hacker lived to be eighty-five, remarried to William Busby of Over Norton, and was buried at Churchill in 1685. The informant against Anne Hacker seems to have been Alice, Lady Moore, widow of the 2nd Viscount Moore of Drogheda, Ireland. Lady Moore was relentless in tracking down recalcitrant royalists. On 5th March 1650 at least ten other Churchill people were summoned before the Committee for Compounding – Giles Harris, George Moorecroft junior, Richard Brayne, Thomas Sessions, John Taplin, Thomas Bridges, Katherine White (widow), William Bridges, John Whitley, and, two days later, Henry Harris. Not all these were necessarily fined, but their ability to pay was assessed on the value of their estate. Giles Harris's personal estate, now occupied by his widow, was valued at £3,000, Richard Brayne at £20 p.a. real estate and £500 personal estate, Morecroft's at £100, Bridges at £90, Sessions at £80 and so on down to Katherine White whose personal estate was at £20. Henry Harris, another of Lady Moore's special victims, 'confesses that he was in arms against Parliament, and begs to compound'. He was fined £30.

---

13 'The Papers of Captain Henry Stevens', ORS Vol. XLII, 1961

Even before the First Civil War had formally ended at Stow-on-the-Wold (26th March 1646), on 28th November 1645, Sir William Walter of Sarsden was singled out for special punishment for 'delinquency in assisting the King'. In 1644 he had lent the king £421 – 1s – 6d. In his defence he alleged that 'for 2½ years [he] has refused all employments in that behalf, and submits on the propositions of Parliament. His estate was worth £800 a year, of which £100 a year is secured to the Church. It is not now worth more than ¼ of that sum, and he has six small children'. On 21st May 1646 he again came before the Committee, complaining that the County Committee on 10th May 1646 made an inventory of his estate, 'with a view to sequester it'. On 9th July he was fined £1,430, but seems to have been allowed to retain his property. The parishioners of Kingham later indignantly submitted a bill to Parliament for damages suffered from the notorious Major George Purefoy during the period in which he was Governor of the Parliamentary Garrison at Compton House (Wynyates) and raided widely throughout the surrounding area.

David Walter of Wolvercote also did not enjoy a good war. In 1644 he was appointed High Sheriff of Oxfordshire by King Charles. But as the royalist garrison of Oxford evacuated the city and fled towards the north to their final defeat at the Battle of Naseby, he set fire to his house at Godstow (23rd May) to prevent it from falling into the hands of the parliamentary forces. In fact they were able to occupy and use what was left of the building.

The period from 1646 to 1662 saw several important changes in church life that affected everyone in the country. Bishops and the Prayer Book were abolished, and a long and boring Presbyterian order of service was enacted but was probably not much used in country villages, and not at all after 1648. After the Civil War, many royalist clergy were ejected from their parishes locally – Kingham, Evenlode, Oddington, Wigginton, Bourton-on-the-Water and others in 1646; Long Compton in 1647, Charlbury and Stow-on-the-Wold in 1648. Benjamin Glyn survived till 1651/2 when he seems tactfully to have withdrawn (there is no record of his ejection) and Thomas Barlow, librarian of the Bodleian Library in Oxford, was 'intruded' in his place. Almost alone in this district, John Nant, the Vicar of Bledington, kept his head down and successfully survived all the changes from 1636 to 1669 – a local Vicar of Bray, quietly performing his underpaid pastoral duties in disregard of the constant ecclesiastical changes. After the Restoration and the Act of Uniformity in 1662, Bishops and the Prayer Book were restored, and clergy who could prove that they had been unjustly evicted were restored to their parishes. Others, like Stephen Ford, the Vicar of Chipping Norton, felt that they could not conform with the Prayer Book, and resigned or were ejected. Still others, like the militant Puritan Thomas Jackson, Rector of Kingham, found that their consciences now allowed them to be episcopally ordained and formally inducted into the parish where they had ministered for many years.

Benjamin Glyn was re-instated as Perpetual Vicar and Lecturer of Churchill by the Bishop of Oxford on 7th February 1662/3, and four months later George Vernon was inducted as Rector of Sarsden. Benjamin Glyn's wife, Hester, was buried in Churchill in October 1681, and there are records of the baptism of four of their children: Benjamin in 1648, Mary in 1651, Phebe in 1659 and Sarah in 1663 – Mary and Phebe's names being inserted irregularly in the register as their baptisms occurred during the period when their father was ejected. Young Benjamin Glyn (1648-1728) can probably be identified with 'Mr Justice Glyn' whose name occurs in several local government documents of the 1680s. His father, Benjamin Glyn the vicar, died on 29th May 1697 and was buried in the old church, aged eighty-four, having spent almost the whole of his long life in the parish where he served, nominally at least, for fifty-four years – longer than any other Churchill incumbent on record.

During the later seventeenth century, two Lecturers, who should perhaps be thought of as Curates of Churchill, can be identified. One was Thomas Barlow (1607-1691) who was Bodley's Librarian in 1652 when he became Lecturer of Churchill. Subsequently he became Provost of Queen's College (1657), Lady Margaret Professor of Divinity at Oxford (1660), and then, reconciling himself to the new regime, Bishop of Lincoln in 1675, although it is unlikely that he ever visited his diocese. He was notorious for having 'trimmed' his sails to all the ecclesiastical changes that occurred until his death in 1691, including those of the brief era of the catholic James II from 1685-1688 when

Barlow published a book 'Plain Reasons why a Protestant of the Church of England should not turn Roman Catholic', – conveniently timed to coincide with James's deposition. Thomas Barlow is still remembered today as the original author of the wording of the oath required from anyone wishing to become a reader in the Bodleian Library

The other Lecturer of Churchill was Stephen Penton, instituted on 4th May 1677, a former pupil of Winchester School and a Fellow of New College, Oxford, who was Principal of St Edmund Hall from 1675 to 1684 and thereafter Principal of Hart Hall, Oxford, and Rector of Glympton. He also published a pamphlet in 1688 entitled 'The Guardian's Instruction or the Gentleman's Romance' which was a thoughtful examination of the advantages of the university tutorial system, then in its infancy. The title 'Lecturer of Churchill' recurs from time to time in the eighteenth century Churchill records.

George Morecroft, eldest son of the royalist Rector of Kingham, acquired the old manor house of Churchill in the mid-seventeenth century (perhaps also with the lordship of the manor). At his death, three men – Edward Powys, Roberte Castell and Thomas Bridges – made a long and detailed inventory of all his personal property, as was required before probate would be granted. On 8th January 1668/9 these three appraisers worked conscientiously through the rooms and outbuildings, and thereby provided us with the means of making a hypothetical reconstruction of what the manor house was like. It had two cellars – the inner cellar and the outward cellar; on the ground floor: the Hall, the Great Parler (parlour), the Little Parler, the kitchen and the larder; on the second floor: the Chamber over the Great Parler, the Chamber within the Parler Chamber, The Chamber over the Little Parler, the Chamber over the Kitchen and the Maides Chamber; outside: the dayrie house and the stable. And also, but not named, almost certainly a barn and a granary. Altogether, this was an imposing house, with six hearths (listed in 1662).

# THE GREAT FIRE OF 1684

The Restoration government of Charles II, always short of funds, introduced the Hearth Tax in 1662, often known as 'chimney money'. Householders, except for the very poor, paid a tax of two shillings a year, in two instalments, for every hearth or fire-place they possessed. The liability to pay was often assessed simply by counting chimneys. The Hearth Tax return for Churchill listed forty-eight dwelling houses, of which fourteen, having fewer than three hearths, were discharged from paying 'by poverty'. The largest house – presumably the ancient manor house – had six hearths and was occupied by Elizabeth Morecroft, the widow of George Morecroft. Thomas Castle, Giles Medcroft and Thomas Mullington had five hearths each, John Braine, William Sessions and William 'Webbdefassett' (William Webb of Foscott?) had four and the remaining inhabitants had two or three. The poorest inhabitants having only one hearth each were Richard La[r]dner, Richard Sparries, Ann Bridges (widow), Susan Hunt (widow), Thomas Reeve and Michaell Hall. These figures would suggest a population of 250 – 300 in 1662. By contrast, only eleven hearths were listed for Sarsden, headed by Sir William Walter whose splendid house contained twenty-four hearths. Edmund Chamberlaine, the Constable who submitted the return, had five hearths, George Farmer and Francis Mancell had four each, and William Beard, Margarett Church (widow) and William Box were discharged by poverty.

The cottages were timber-framed, thatched, and frequently single-storey. As such, they were very vulnerable to fire, as occurred in London in 1666. On Wednesday, 30th July 1684, a disastrous fire swept through the old village of Churchill. A strong wind carried the flames through the densely-packed buildings. Twenty houses were destroyed, as well as many barns and outbuildings, and this probably included the old vicarage adjacent to the church since a 'terrier' of church land, dated 1722, includes a reference to the land 'on which the Vicarage formerly stood'. The fire, that began in John Box's house, was allegedly caused 'by the Covetuousness of an Old Woman, who to save the expense of Chimney-money, and being by trade a Baker, had made a Funnel from her Oven into another Chimney'. The fire lasted four hours and 'four people were Kill'd, two by falling of the Ruines, and two Burnt'.

Seventeen householders in Churchill brought a petition to the Oxfordshire Quarter Sessions to secure the issue of a Brief, by royal mandate. A Church Brief could be issued to request donations towards some worthy cause; it was read by the parish clerk in every church on Sunday after the end of the service; a collection would be taken and handed by the churchwardens to the travelling collector. In this case, the Brief would probably have been issued by the Diocese of Oxford and read throughout all the parish churches in the diocese. In those days, collections were not normally taken up in church unless requested for some specific object. It is unlikely that the total amount of £1,800 was raised, but perhaps sufficient to alleviate the suffering of the dispossessed householder.

The total cost of the fire came to £1799 – 15s 11d, as valued by John Hacker, Gentleman, on the oaths of six village craftsmen, William Watson, Richard Clift and Richard Ford, masons, and Robert Kyte, William Fletcher and James Izard, carpenters. The size of the buildings destroyed was calculated by counting the number of 'bays' affected. The word 'bay' was customarily used to convey the size of a house; a bay was the width between each section of the house, and could have been separately constructed. Small cottages would have consisted of one bay, whereas a large house might extend to as many as six. In the case of Churchill, one hundred and eighty seven bays were destroyed, and eight years later there were still one hundred waiting to be rebuilt. Warden Woodward's contemporary (1659-1674) Progress Notes have several references to the grant of elm trees from the manorial land in Kingham for building extra bays to houses there, for example, on 26th July 1671 five elms were granted to the Widow Huckins to build three bays of her dwelling house. These appear to have been full-grown trees, so five mature trees were required to construct three bays. By extrapolation, the rebuilding of Churchill would have required over three hundred mature trees, a significant deforestation of the parish. This must partly explain why the newly-rebuilt village was constructed chiefly of stone: fewer trees were needed, and stone buildings were, of course, less flammable.

The valuation of the properties destroyed gives an indication of the burdens taken by each householder:

|  |  |  |  | Bays |
|---|---|---|---|---|
| William Joyner | £209 | 5s | 0d | 21 |
| Thomas Bignell | £196 | 9s | 4d | 20 |
| John Box | £188 | 14s | 3d | 19 |
| Christopher Hunt | £175 | 6s | 0d | 18 |
| John Barrett | £151 | 4s | 3d | 15 |
| Robert Gunne | £111 | 6s | 6d | 11 |
| Anthony Newman | £101 | 15s | 0d | 10 |
| Jonathan Jett | £98 | 10s | 10d | 10 |
| Walter Norton | £97 | 6s | 8d | 10 |
| William Bridges | £92 | 12s | 0d | 9 |
| Thomas Shurley | £84 | 2s | 8d | 9 |
| William Brooks | £83 | 13s | 0d | 9 |
| Thomas Spurrier | £63 | 14s | 2d | 7 |
| Christopher Guy | £60 | 5s | 0d | 6 |
| John Jett  (barn) | £25 | 17s | 4d | 3 |
| William Horseman | £16 | 12s | 6d | 2 |
| Walter Mathewes | £15 | 15s | 4d | 2 |
| Thomas Castell | £14 | 7s | 11d | 2 |
| John Rymehill | £7 | 0s | 0d | 1 |
| Richard Edwards  (barn) | £2 | 15s | 0d | 1 |
| Margarett Jett | £1 | 13s | 2d | 1 |
| John Cross | £1 | 10s | 0d | 1 |

In all, 187 bays or small buildings were destroyed, and the total cost was calculated at £1799 – 15s – 11d. as stated. It would be hard to overestimate the impact that the fire made on the whole parish. There was no national Fire Insurance scheme before 1710, so the cost to those who had lost their homes, agricultural buildings and all their domestic property would have to be carried by the families involved or they would have to rely on the charity of friends and relatives elsewhere, unless they could obtain a Brief.

Twenty parishioners were affected by the loss of their homes and property. The village made an application through their magistrates to the Oxfordshire Quarter Sessions who in turn submitted a certificate authorising Chancery to issue a Brief, and the certificate was entrusted to Sir William Walter who secured the Letters Patent required by the Court of Chancery. At that point, the Keeper of the Great Seal (Lord Guilford) died and was succeeded by the notorious Judge Jeffries who decided to reject the petition from Churchill. The poor householders had now to wait a further five years until the Revolution of 1688 overthrew James II and Lord Jeffries as well. Unfortunately, it was then discovered that Judge Jeffries had lost the original certificate, so the whole process had to be recommenced. At Easter, 1692, eight years after the fire, a fresh petition from 'several poor inhabitants of Churchill' was submitted to Quarter Sessions, and the certificate renewed.

After this disaster, the village was gradually rebuilt in stone closer to the crest of the hill.

# THE CHARITY SCHOOLS

If perhaps the old vicarage was destroyed in the fire of 1684, Benjamin Glyn was the last vicar to live in that medieval house. The churchyard was extended to include the former vicarage garden, and the present ornamental gateway was then erected.

After the great fire of Churchill, the next vicar, James Butterworth, appears to have lived at first in Sarsden, perhaps in Sarsden House. But Sarsden House itself was destroyed by a fire on 6th November 1689 and was rebuilt during the next five years at a cost of £20,000. Butterworth then bought for himself the property subsequently known as Warren Hastings House where he was living when he made his will in 1707. He was a Lancashire man, and a bachelor, and his will is concerned chiefly with the disposal of his property in Rochdale. However, he bequeathed 'unto my servant Thomas Watts the Younger' the house 'wherein I now inhabit with the backside and Orchard thereunto adjoining and belonging and also my one halfe yard land and one halfe part of halfe a quarter of a yard land in Churchill aforesaid with the Messuage and lands I purchased of Richard Prew and Francis Corbett, and also all other my lands … in Churchill … to the said Thomas Watts whom I make sole executor of this my will …' Well done, thou good and faithful servant. If a yardland can still be estimated at approximately thirty acres, Thomas Watts will have acquired not far short of twenty acres as well as a substantial house. During James Butterworth's time the chancel of the church was restored; the date of the restoration can still be discerned high on the east wall. Perhaps the church, too, had been damaged in the great fire.

The Walter family continued to preside over the village until 1731. Sir John Walter held the advowsons of Sarsden and Churchill, together with the right to present the Lecturer of Churchill and conveyed these rights to three Trustees. In 1724 the Trustees were Sir John Stonehouse, Sir Robert Jenkinson and Mr Rowney; in 1738 they were Mr Rowney, Mr Henry Perrot of Barnsley and North Leigh, and the Revd Theophilus Leigh of Broadwell and Adlestrop.

Anne Walter, an elderly and eccentric spinster, granddaughter of Sir John, daughter of Sir William and aunt of Sir John Walter, was convinced that she would one day be murdered. Therefore, in her will she made provision for £600 to be spent in tracking down and apprehending her murderer. If, however, by accident she were to die a natural death, the money was to be applied, in accordance with her alternative instructions '*for the maintenance and education of poor girls under the age of twenty years who shall be educated in the doctrine of the church of England and born in the parish of Sarsden and Churchill … and when the said poor girls shall come to the age of twenty years and are capable of being confirmed then the Minister of Sarsden and Churchill … shall carry them to the Bishop of the Diocese to be confirmed and upon each of them being confirmed by the Bishop such poor girl … shall receive ten pounds'*. Anne Walter, of course, died peaceably in her bed in 1707 and so the money was duly employed in the establishment of Churchill Charity School, better known as Anne Walter's School. A further £600 derived from the rent of property in Ascott-under-Wychwood was used to fit out girls for domestic service. This was the origin of Anne Walter's Trust, a self-perpetuating group of local gentry and clergy who administered the funds.

The trust was generous and seems to have been well-administered. Very fortunately, the long-lost original minute book of the Trust, that recorded the annual accounts and the decision of the annual Trustees' Meeting, has recently re-emerged and been acquired by Mrs Joy Timms who has very generously permitted me to make transcripts of some of the pages and to use them in this account. From them, it appears that the school and house for the schoolmistress were built in the year 1713-14. Sir John Walter provided the site, and William Clift, the Churchill mason and builder, erected the buildings. Unfortunately, the figures for expenditure on this year's account have been lost, but they included payments to William Joyner the carpenter, John Paty of Chipping Norton for planks and freestone, John Hyatt the slater for the roof, Lovell the painter, Freeman the smith for casements (windows), Weston the ironmonger for locks, Thomas Lardner the carpenter and William Freeman for the pumps, and Robert Brooks for transporting the stone. To give the edifice a final touch of gentility, Mr Powell the surveyor was paid for 'the Coat of Arms etc.' The provision of an outhouse with pumps suggests that there were adequate toilet facilities. The total cost would seem to have been £164 – 19s – 4d, which was more than covered from the rents of lands bequeathed to the Trust, and was settled by August 1718. The plaque on the wall inside the old school 'Anne Walter's Hall' read: *'To the glory of God and the Increase of Christian Piety. Anne Walter, daughter of Sir William Walter of Sarsden, Bart., Aunt of the present Sir John Walter, founded this school with an endowment of six hundred pounds For the liberall education of Poor Girls of the Parishes of Sarsden and Churchill In the Year of our Lord 1716'.* Poor Anne Walter! Mrs Rose tells us that the memorial tablet that she had had cut for herself during her lifetime was misappropriated by one of her trustees who reversed it, had an inscription made in his own honour, and erected in a church in Somerset.

The first schoolmistress appointed was Mrs Underhill, who, in addition to her house, was paid a salary of £10 with the addition of £1 for fuel, paid six-monthly on Lady Day and Michaelmas. This was a generous salary at that time, and the Trustees could afford to employ a satisfactory teacher. There is no record of the death of Mrs Underhill, but by 1726 the Schoolmistress was Mrs Stone. By 1734 Mrs Hyat appears to have been the schoolmistress, and Thomas Mander was paid a salary of one guinea a year, probably for acting as school accountant and secretary. Mrs Capps was schoolmistress in 1746 and Mrs Bowel in 1782. There is no reference in the eighteenth century accounts to an assistant mistress.

By comparing a list of the children who were educated in the school on 8th September 1720 with the entries in the Churchill baptismal register, it is possible to calculate the age-range of the girls:

| Baptism at Churchill | | Name | Age (at least) |
|---|---|---|---|
| 19th May | 1706 | Elizabeth, daughter of Thomas Temple | 14.3 |
| 7th January | 1706/7 | Frances, daughter of Henry Medcroft | 13.8 |
| 18th July | 1708 | Frances, daughter of Thomas Temple | 12.2 |
| 29th August | 1708 | Sarah, daughter of William Joyner | 12.0 |
| 5th December | 1708 | Anne, daughter of Henry Boulter | 11.9 |
| 31st July | 1709 | Mary, daughter of Thomas Sherburn | 11.1 |
| 27th December | 1709 | Dinah, daughter of George Grimmett | 10.8 |
| 7th January | 1710/1 | Mary, daughter of John and Margaret Newman | 9.8 |
| 6th July | 1712 | Elizabeth, daughter of George Grimmett | 8.2 |
| 16th November | 1712 | Sarah, daughter of George Horseman | 7.10 |
| 31st May | 1713 | Elizabeth, daughter of Henry Boulter | 7.3 |
| 17th October | 1714 | Mary, daughter of George Horseman | 5.11 |
| 20th February | 1714/5 | Mary, daughter of Thomas Larner | 5.7 |

Not baptised at Churchill:

Mary, daughter of Richard Baker

Elizabeth, daughter of Richard Baker

Anne, daughter of John Newman

Girls from Sarsden:

> Rose, daughter of Thomas Meadcroft
>
> Joan, daughter of St[even] Hanks
>
> Joan, daughter of Henry Box
>
> Sarah, daughter of Henry Box
>
> Mary, daughter of Rue[ben] Sheppard
>
> Sarah, daughter of Rue[ben] Sheppard

This gives us a total of twenty-two girls, with ages ranging from five to fourteen years. A similar list in 1761 names twenty-five girls aged from five to sixteen years. In this case the two oldest girls, Dillon Hughes and Sarah Robinson, will have been Pupil Teachers. It cannot have been easy for the schoolmistress to handle such a wide age-range in a single class. A due time after entering the school the girls were formally admitted and 'Cloathed', provided with a gown and pinafore. The gowns (in 1782) were made in the village, and cost one shilling each. On leaving the school each girl was presented with a Bible, a Book of Common Prayer 'and the singing,' and 'The Whole Duty of Man' – a pious devotional book published in 1658, and probably written by Richard Allestree, Provost of Eton. The book contains seventeen discourses, mainly on matters of Christian morals and, after the Bible and Pilgrim's Progress, was the third best-selling book of that time. I doubt whether any girl ever read her copy. Presumably the 'singing' was the new version of the metrical Psalms published by Tate and Brady in 1698 ('Through all the changing scenes of life' has survived into modern hymnbooks). The cost of these books – the Bibles at 5s 6d each, the 'Whole Duties` at five shillings each, and 'Primers' at 1s 3d each – formed one of the more substantial items in the annual accounts. The Primers were apparently spelling books devised by 'Dixon, the Schoolmaster of the Bath'. The girls were taught to read and write, to do very simple arithmetic, to sew and learn other crafts that would be useful for a domestic servant and a housewife, to know the Bible and Prayer Book, and to learn by heart the Catechism and the Collect for the coming week. There is no evidence that any girl was given her ten pounds on her wedding day. On completing her education, the girls were formally 'Dismissed' from the school.

A sample of the minutes of the Trustees' meeting is taken from 1727:

*Att a Meetinge of the Trustees for the Charity School of Churchill Aprill the 9th 1727.*

> *Imp's Elizabeth Smith, Elizabeth Boulter, Elizabeth Lardner, and Catherine Barnett having been Educated in the sd School for a Due time were then dismissed out of the sd School, and that each of them shall have a Bible with the Common Prayer bound up with it and a Book Called the Whole Duty of Man.*

> *Item: It is ordered and agreed that Ann Nash and Elizabeth Clift two children in the close [?] shall from hence forth be Discharged and dismissed out of the sd School for not comeing to the sd School in [dresses] and being very uncleanly.*

> *Item: it is ordered and directed that Elizabeth Cowly, Elizabeth Garden, Ann Horseman, Elizabeth Carter, Mary Clift, Mary Widdows, Mary Day, Elizabeth Harryson, Ann Widdows, & Harriet Hale shall be Cloathed.*

> *Item: it is directed and ordered That six books the Whole Duty of Man and six Bibles with the Common Prayer bound up with it shall be provided.*

> *Item: it is agreed and ordered that Mary Newman, Elizabeth Cowly, Mary Grimmet, Elizabeth Harvey, Rachele Hunt & Elizabeth Gibbs shall be taken into the School & Educated.*

> *[Sgd]*  *Rob: Walter*  *Will Shepperd*
>      *R.B.Jenkinson* *Tho: Pursell*
>      *Jona: Cope*   *Robt. Brooks*

Churchill was a fortunate village to have such a school. It was well-built and maintained, and the Schoolmistresses were paid enough to ensure that they were competent and respectable. There were then over 1,200 charity schools in England, but mostly in the towns, and more than half of them were for boys only. The average number of pupils in these schools was less than twenty-five, so Churchill Charity School was slightly smaller.

An early nineteenth century Gazeteer, referring to the school, says, somewhat misleadingly, that 'the girls are partly cloathed' and that the Vicar has the heavy burden of 'carrying' them to the Bishop for Confirmation. In 1825, the Charity Commissioners reported on Anne Walter's School that

> *A salary of twenty guineas per annum is paid to the mistress, and about £20 per annum is applied to the purchase of clothes for scholars. There are always twenty-four girls in the school, who are admitted at the age of from seven to nine, and are allowed to remain four years. They are taught reading, writing and accounts, with knitting and needlework, and are supplied with gowns, bonnets and other articles of clothing. They are also supplied with Bibles and Prayer-books on leaving school and are confirmed when of proper age.*[14]

Anne Walter's School survived into the twentieth century when it became part of the C. of E. Primary School. Anne Walter's imaginary murderer never knew what a boon he was unwittingly conferring on the girls of the village, but Anne Walter would have been justly proud that her wishes had been so effectively discharged.

Elizabeth Vernon, who married Sir John Walter (1673-1722), remarried to Lord Harcourt of Stanton Harcourt (c.1661 – 1727), a well-known and wealthy lawyer who had briefly been Lord Chancellor from 1713-1714, but outlived him by more than twenty years. She continued to take an active interest in Sarsden and Churchill where she followed Anne Walter's example by providing for the education of ten boys.

> *There are ten Boys kept at School by the Lady Dowager Harcourt; they are cloath'd every year, taught to say their Catechism, and*

---

14   Ref: Henderson, op. cit., p.192.

*some of them to write. And when they leave the School they have each of them a Bible, Common Prayer Book, and Whole Duty of Man given them. For which she allows ten pounds ten shillings a year*

(Nathaniel Sturges: Visitation Return 1738)

No premises were provided for Lady Harcourt's school, and it was less well-endowed than Anne Walter's school. Pupils may have been taught in the schoolmaster's house or in the church. Most boys did not remain at school much beyond the age of seven after which they were expected to earn a few extra pence for the family income by scaring birds in the fields. Pupils expected to learn to read, but only the older and brighter boys would have been taught to write.

This school must have survived Lady Harcourt's death in 1748, and may have been attended by Warren Hastings in the 1730s and by William Smith in the 1770s for he tells us that 'there were two [schools] in the village (but one only for little children)'.

Kingham also had a charity school, maintained at the expense of the rector, during much of the eighteenth century, but it disappeared when a new rector discontinued his support.

In her will (dated 1736, proved 1748) the Viscountess Harcourt left £200 to Queen Anne's Bounty[15] for the augmentation of the Vicarage of Churchill.

---

15  In 1704 Queen Anne set up a fund from the First Fruits and Tenths – ecclesiastical taxes that had been confiscated by Henry VIII and that she had inherited as Supreme Governor of the Church of England. This money was used to augment the livings of the least well-endowed parishes in England. It was ultimately subsumed by the Church Commissioners

# JOHN GRIFFIN THE NON-JUROR

There was much excitement in Churchill at one o'clock on Tuesday, 9th January 1705, when a group of men ploughing in the field witnessed a 'wonderful Prodigy in the sky'. According to one of the men, Daniel Flaxney, they saw 'three Strange things, all of which was to be seen about a Quarter of an Hour, and some part of it near half an Houre. It was the appearance of four Suns, beside the true Sun, the east side of the Sky being then indifferent clear, but on the West side there were some Clouds'. In addition they saw in the heavens 'Steams, Circles and Crosses' – 'firy', 'rainbow', 'blewish white' and 'chrystal'. Four men (Thomas Davis, Robert Davis, Robert Brooks and John Smith) later added their names to Daniel Flaxney's 'to testify that this above is true'. The heavenly apparition was taken to be 'prodigies ... sent for signs to Mankind', and received passing national interest when printed on one of those flysheets that circulated in London, although what portentous event they were taken to foreshadow is unclear, as 1705 was a year signally devoid of public or local interest, unless it were the laying of the foundation stone for Blenheim Palace, or the arrival of John Griffin in Churchill later that year.

At the entrance to the old church (Churchill Heritage Centre) there is a beautifully inscribed ornamental marble floor slab commemorating John Griffin. John Griffin came to Sarsden to be curate to George Vernon in 1705. Born in Towcester in 1680, he had graduated from Merton College, Oxford, in 1702 and been ordained priest by the Bishop of Oxford in 1704. After a brief curacy at Compton in Kent, he came to Sarsden and subscribed to the statutory declaration on 11th October 1705. He would at that time have taken the Oath of Supremacy acknowledging that Queen Anne was the Supreme Governor of the Church of England. He probably took over the day-to-day running of the parish from George Vernon (1637-1720), who was occupied in his other parish at Bourton-on-the-Water (where he is buried), and recorded in the Sarsden parish register various gifts made to the church there. Robert Walter, the youngest son of Sir William Walter of Sarsden House, was the same age as John Griffin and no doubt the two young men found enough in common to form the basis of their life-long friendship. James Butterworth, the Vicar of Churchill, died on 3rd May 1710, but at least three months earlier John Griffin had been signing the Churchill register as curate. On 27th July 1712, John Griffin made his formal subscription to the Thirty-nine Articles of Religion and to obedience to the Bishop of Oxford on being admitted as Lecturer of Churchill. This subscription is still preserved in the Oxford diocesan archives, and is written in a neat and efficient hand:

*I John Griffin Master of Arts being to be admitted as Lecturer of Churchill in the Diocese of Oxon do willingly subscribe to the three Articles contained in the 36th Canon. Witness my hand the 27th day of July 1712.*

[sgd] John Griffin

*I John Griffin do declare that I will conform to the liturgy of the Church of England as it is now by Law established. Witness my Hand the Day and Year abovewritten.*

[sgd] John Griffin

It is ironical that the only vicar of Churchill whose written declaration of conformity has been preserved was also to be the only one openly to break with the authority and liturgy of the church. There is no evidence that he was presented as vicar, although he was later to be described as Vicar of Churchill, and his curacy of the parish conveniently bridges the gap between James Butterworth and Nathaniel Sturges. During the eighteenth century the terms 'vicar` and 'lecturer' seem to have been used interchangeably in Churchill.

After the death of Queen Anne (1714), John Griffin had scruples of conscience about the legality of the accession of King George of

Hanover. He had, of course, been too young to be personally involved in the earlier Non-Juror repudiation of William III in 1688, and had therefore not been required to subscribe to the Oaths of Supremacy in 1689, 1696 and 1702. In 1689, nine bishops and about four hundred clergy – about 4% of the total – had refused to take the oath and in consequence had been deprived of their parish livings. Although most High Churchmen were satisfied with the Anglican Church under Queen Anne, and although both the main political parties accepted the accession of King George I in 1714, there was an uncomfortable awareness of the superior claim to the throne by Queen Anne's half-brother, James, 'The Old Pretender`, even though as a staunch Roman Catholic he was disqualified by the Act of Settlement (1701). Aware of the growing unrest that culminated in the Jacobite Rebellion of 1715, Parliament decided to ensure the reliability of the armed forces, civilian office-holders and clergy by re-enacting the Oath of Abjuration which was designed to expose and discredit Roman Catholics and political Jacobites, as the followers of the exiled Old Pretender were called. An unintended consequence of this requirement was that some clergy, conscientiously aware of their obligation of allegiance to the natural heir to the throne, felt unable to take the oath of allegiance to George I. When this oath was administered to the clergy, John Griffin was obliged to reconsider his loyalties and felt that in all conscience he was unable to conform. In consequence, he refused the oath and automatically forfeited both his posts as Curate of Sarsden and Lecturer (or Vicar) of Churchill. Oxford University was on fire with Jacobitism. Thomas Hearne, the Oxford antiquarian, who as a Jacobite himself had been forced to resign from the Bodleian Library, recorded that 'Mr Griffin, Minister of Sarsden, who went out M.A. of Merton, hath thrown up his living'. John Griffin accepted the appointment as private chaplain to Lord Plymouth.

At this point it was logical for John Griffin to seek admission to the Church of the Non-Jurors, but he was not received into membership until 18th March 1719/20, when he was formally admitted by Bishop Brett. The Non-Jurors were not part of the Church of England but nor were they Roman Catholics; in 1694 the exiled King James II had kindly approved the consecration of two priests as Non-Juror Bishops. John

Griffin moved to London where on 25<sup>th</sup> November 1722 he himself was consecrated as a Non-Juror Bishop at Mr Collier's Oratory in Red Lion Street, Holborn, by Bishops Jeremy Collier, Archibald Campbell and Thomas Brett. After the defeat of the Jacobites in 1715, they rapidly lost influence and the Non-Juror Church was declining in numbers. Their historian says that 'in many ways [Griffin] was one of the most distinguished of the late Non-Juror Bishops. He had a strong sense of the responsibilities of the Episcopal office, and ... rendered very considerable service to the cause'. In 1728 he accepted the charge of the Non-Juror congregation at Newcastle-upon-Tyne, but the dwindling numbers of Non-Jurors led to them being increasingly isolated. To make matters worse, the Non-Jurors began to quarrel among themselves and form factions over trivial disputes in the wording of the liturgy for the Eucharist. Griffin joined the party called the 'Usagers' who wished to turn back to the Prayer Book of 1549 and to revive four discontinued usages in the communion service – all of which have today become acceptable to the modern Church of England, but were at that time considered to be dangerously 'Popish`.

By 1730, John Griffin, although still only aged fifty, was seriously ill, 'quite drowned in dropsy and in a very weak condition`. In this state he made his last long journey back from Newcastle to Sarsden House to be the guest of his old friend, Sir Robert Walter. His last letter was written and dated from Sarsden on 5<sup>th</sup> July 1731. Three days later he died and was buried on 9<sup>th</sup> July in the middle of the chancel of the old church at Churchill where as a young man he had administered the sacraments. The marble slab there recorded the burial of the remains of 'John Griffin, Master of Arts, a pious and erudite man'. It is pleasing to observe the tolerance that welcomed him home to his old parish and accorded him dignity in burial, although of course there was no reference in the burial register or on his grave to indicate his illegal Episcopal title. Four months later, his friend Sir Robert Walter died, the last male member of the Walters of Sarsden House; he and John Griffin were both aged fifty-one.

# NATHANIEL STURGES

It is probable that Benjamin Glyn, who died in 1697, had been the last resident Vicar of Churchill. The wording of Anne Walter's will a few years later suggests that by that time the benefices of Sarsden and Churchill had effectively been combined, although a separate Vicarage of Churchill was briefly revived towards the end of the eighteenth century. Nathaniel Sturges, from Sudbury in Derbyshire, who was Rector of Sarsden from 1720 to 1762, described himself as Minister of Churchill during that period. Much of the work of the parish at that time must have been done by the Parish Clerks such as Giles Harris, William Gardener and William Mullington, who were laymen, and by a series of Curates, some of whom were also the incumbents of other parishes. The registers preserve the names of several such ephemeral curates: John Phillips, John Tucker, Simon Paget and Thomas Johnes.

The old church must still have been serviceable, for in 1715 a new cushion was provided for the pulpit Bible and was first used on Good Friday. The registers record other furnishings:

*Oct 20th 1720 A Great Bible and Common Prayer Book in English of the Oxford edition were provided at the charge of Sir John Walter, Bart., and given to the parish church of Churchill. Witness my hand: N. Sturges, Minister of Churchill.*

*Nov 20th 1720 a new Surplice was provided at the expense of the Parish and brought into the church for the use of the same. Witness my hand: N.Sturges, Minister of Churchill.*

*Sep 26th 1724 A large Silver Chalice with a cover was given to the Parish Church of Churchill by the Lady Walter, Relict of Sir John*

*Walter, Bart., deceased and was delivered to the Churchwardens to be kept for the use of thesame. Witness my hand: N. Sturges Min'r of Churchill.*

*The Register for the Parish of Churchill, November the First 1754. This book was committed to my care by the Revd Mr Nathaniel Sturges, Rector of Sarsden. Witness my hand: Sim: Paget Nov 1 1754.*

This was the new marriage register that every parish was required to purchase in accordance with Hardwicke's Marriage Act, and which had been bought for Churchill Parish by Giles Harris. Simon Paget was by then the 'Curate in Charge'.

In 1738, Dr Thomas Secker (Bishop of Oxford 1737-1758) required all his clergy to respond to a series of questions concerning their parishes and their work. Since this was instead of a personal visit by the Bishop, the responses are known as a Visitation Return. Nathaniel Sturges made separate returns for Churchill and Sarsden, and these throw much light on the life of the parishes during the eighteenth century. The return for Churchill says:

*The parish is betwixt three and four miles in length and about one and a half miles in breadth. There is no other village [within the parish], only one house in a neighbouring village belonging to it. It contains fourscore and eight houses but there is no family of note in it.*

*There is no Papist, Quaker or Dissenter of any sort in the Parish.*

*There are no persons who profess to disregard Religion, or who commonly absent themselves from Church on the Lord's Day.*

*I reside at Sarsden but half a mile distant, and supply both places myself.*

*Publick Service is duly perform'd every Lord's Day, and one sermon preach'd. And there are usually prayers on Saints Days. I hear the Children their Catechism in Lent, but have not time to expound it for reason given under the same Article for Sarsden. There are four Sacraments in a year, and sometimes fifty or sixty persons at a Sacrament ...*

*There is a free School founded by Mrs Anne Walter for Girls of the Parishes of Churchill and Sarsden. The number is left to the discretion of the Governors who are Gentlemen in the neighbourhood, and the Revenue in Land is £24 – 0s – 0d. The School Mistress teaches them to work, read and say their Catechism, and they are cloath'd yearly, as far as the mony will hold out.*

*There are ten Boys kept at School by the Lady Dowager Harcourt, they are cloath'd every year, taught to say their Catechism, and some of them to write. And when they leave the School they have each of them a Bible, Common Prayer Book, and Whole Duty of Man given them. For which she allows ten pounds ten shillings a year.*

*There are one hundred and fifteen pounds plac'd out at Interest, £50 given by Mr Edmund Wansell and £20 by Mr Richard Hacker. (The other Benefactors are not known.) The interest is dispos'd of yearly among the Poor of the Parish.*

*The money given at the Offertory is dispos'd of by the Minister and Church Wardens to the Poor of the Parish, and chiefly to those who were at Sacrament.*

Nat. Sturges, Minister of Churchill

He gave additional information in his return for Sarsden ('Saresden'). This parish was two miles long and half a mile broad, and contained twenty houses and *'a Gentleman's seat belonging to the Walters family... Being obliged to read prayers four times and preach twice [every Sunday], I have not time to expound (the Catechism) to (the children). Twenty come to sacrament. There is £100 placed out at interest, one half left by the Walter family, the other by Mr Edmund Wansell, to be distributed yearly among the Poor of the Parish.*`

In those days it was customary to celebrate Holy Communion not more than three or four times a year – at Easter, Whitsun, Christmas and perhaps Michaelmas. There was always a smaller congregation for Holy Communion. Collections (the offertory) were taken up only at Communion services and, unless otherwise directed by the Bishop, were to be distributed among the poor of the parish.

In his will (made 2nd November 1759), Nathaniel Sturges shows that he held the lease of a house and three Yardlands (about ninety acres) in Churchill, which presumably he sublet for farming. He said also that the late Sir Robert Walter, before he died in 1731, had entrusted to him five portraits of members of the Walter family and requested that they should remain in the Sarsden parsonage house for ever.

'Reverend Mr Sturges Rector of Sarsden' was buried on 15th August 1762. Two years before his death a new vicar was appointed for Churchill – the first since the death of Benjamin Glyn. Robert Woodward was vicar from 1760 to 1768, Walter Thomas from 1768 to 1774 and Charles Tahourdin from 1774 to 1787. Because the stipend available for Churchill was so low, the work of vicar was usually combined with being Rector of Cornwell or Master of Chipping Norton Free Grammar School.

# THE CHURCH ALES

Amongst several attempts at an autobiography and other documents relating to William Smith the geologist, the Oxford University Museum of Geology holds a set of accounts dated between 9th May and 7th June 1721 that the geologist had inherited from his great-grandfather, also called William Smith. Although the entries seem at first cryptic, they refer to the Whitsun Church Ales that were held, probably annually, to raise money for the church. William Smith (senior) appears to have been the Treasurer for the Church Ales, and was meticulous in recording all his expenditure. Cakes and ale were the essential ingredients on such occasions: earthenware cups were hired from Thomas Bradley and the cakes were provided by Thomas Evans, the pastrycook from Kingham. There was even an entry for the purchase of ribbons – if that is what 'rubands` means!

But far more interesting is the list of payments made to the characters in a drama. These include the Lord, the Lady, the Lord's man, the Lady's man, five Maids (Betty Haines, Betty Reeve, Betty Wheeler, Mary Box and Betty Dutton), the Fool (or Squire – both names were used interchangeably), the Fiddler (John Phips), the man who held the treasure box and twenty two other men amongst whom were the six Morris dancers. Morris dancing (that is, Moorish dancing), of course, has great antiquity, but documentary records are few and William Smith's accounts may be the earliest written record of Morris dancing in Oxfordshire. Mike Heaney, the national expert on Morris dancing, told me that 'Whitsun Ales in general were essentially fairs, not "dramas", with stalls, drinking, feasting, dancing &c., presided over by the Lord and Lady and their attendants in a mock court, in which visitors had to know the correct terminology for the various trappings parodying a true court, or pay a forfeit.'[16]

---

16  Personal correspondence, 8th February 1982

The church was ambivalent about Whitsun Ales: on the one hand they were rightly regarded as occasions for drunkenness and immorality; on the other hand, they provided a useful source of income for the church. As a result, they were quietly tolerated. In Churchill, there were also the Youth Ales that immediately followed the Church Ales. And then, in November, came the Church Wake that seems to have been held over three or more days preceding and following 12th November. A wake was originally the vigil preceding a festival, and the choice of date is significant: 12th November was 'Old All Saints Day' the day on which the Feast of All Saints would have been commemorated had not the calendar been changed in 1752, suggesting that the old church – in the absence of other evidence – was indeed dedicated to All Saints. By the eighteenth century, the vigil had largely been superseded by a day of feasting and games. If we can assume that the village also commemorated May Day, with a maypole, garlands and dancing, and bonfire night on 5th November, it can be accepted that life in the eighteenth century was not entirely work and no play. But Christmas Day was little observed in those days.

The church of St James at Sarsden that adjoined Sarsden House was rebuilt in 1760. The Rector of Sarsden after the death of Nathaniel Sturges was the Revd Tilleman Hodgkinson from Woodstock. He was aged thirty-nine when he was instituted and was probably non-resident since in the same year he matriculated as a mature undergraduate at Trinity College, Oxford.

During these years, the advowson of Churchill – the right to nominate a vicar – was purchased by a layman who thereby became the legal Lay Rector of the parish. As well as appointing vicars to Churchill, he was also entitled to receive the payment of the great tithes of the parish. This outrageous situation, properly known as 'impropriation`, was detested by the clergy and much disliked by the farmers who had to pay tithes but received no benefit in return. One such Lay Rector was Augustine Skinner; he in turn sold the advowson to the Rollinson family. When the Lay Rector failed to appoint a vicar, as happened in Churchill in 1768, the responsibility passed to the Crown. But the Lay Rector was not obliged to appoint a vicar: a curate-in-charge or 'perpetual curate` was sufficient, and all too often the canon law that required such curates to be licensed by the bishop was discreetly ignored, thus depriving them of the right to receive the legal minimum stipend and of their security of tenure. Another example of the incredible slackness in the church was the increased number of clergy who held several livings – parishes – often at a considerable distance from each other. The implication, of course, was that the clergyman could live in only one of his parishes and had to employ curates, at a derisory stipend, for his other parishes. Although this – both 'pluralism' and 'non-residence` – were illegal under canon law, a local example was the notorious Dr Thomas Brookes (1732-1814) who managed to be Vicar of Shipton-under-Wychwood (with all its forest hamlets such as Leafield, Milton-under-Wychwood and Lyneham), Perpetual Curate of Ascott-under-Wychwood, Perpetual Curate of Fifield and of Idbury, Rector of Westcote in the Diocese of Gloucester and Rector of Daylesford in the Diocese of Worcester. The Bishop of Oxford described the situation in 1784 as 'shameful', but did nothing about it. The Church of England was desperately in need of reformation.

# WARREN HASTINGS

*Warren Hastings*

*Reproduced by permission of the National Portrait Gallery London*

Nathaniel Sturges was no doubt embarrassed by the presence of a Non-Juror bishop in his parish. But John Griffin was not the only clergyman seeking refuge in Sarsden and Churchill. The Revd Penystone Hastings, Rector of Daylesford, having apparently quarrelled with the lord of his manor, had vacated the parsonage house in Daylesford and come to live in Churchill. Daylesford (at that time a detached parish in the County and Diocese of Worcester) had for centuries belonged to the Hastings family, but in 1715 Penystone's elder brother, Samuel, faced by mounting debts, sold the estate to Jacob Knight, a merchant of Bristol. Penystone Hastings had married Priscilla Gardener, a distant relative, and by 1715 there were four children of the marriage. The rector and his family moved into a substantial well-built house, now known as 'Warren Hastings House' on Hastings Hill. He may have purchased or rented part of this house from its owner, Thomas Watts, to whom it had been bequeathed by James Butterworth, and from this residence he continued to serve his parish of Daylesford. His eldest son, also called Penystone, matriculated at Balliol College, Oxford, in 1724 but did not stay to take a degree. In July 1730 at Worcester he married Hester Warren, the daughter of a yeoman farmer from Twyning in Gloucestershire, and their daughter was born shortly afterwards. At about the same time, young Penystone was ordained a priest, and in

November 1730 he was presented by the Crown as Vicar of Bledington. The living there was impoverished, the vicarage house in ruins, and the appointment was made by the Crown only after the patron had failed to find anyone willing to take on such a neglected parish. Young Pensytone came to Churchill to live with his father, so that by 1732 there were two ordained members of the Hastings family living there – the Rector of Daylesford and the Vicar of Bledington. Despite all the antiquity of the house of Hastings, Nathaniel Sturges felt able to say (in 1738, when Warren Hastings was six years old) that 'no family of note` was living in his parish.

Hester Hastings gave birth to her second child at Churchill on 6th December 1732. Following the custom of the time, he was given his mother's maiden name – Warren – as his Christian name. His mother died within a week of giving birth to her only son. While his daughter-in-law lay dead or dying in his house, and his new-born grandson was only five days old, the Rector of Daylesford wrote a lengthy letter to Dr Thomas Nash, historian of Worcestershire, in which he derived the pedigree of the Hastings family from one 'Hastings the Dane'. For some reason, the baptism of the infant Warren Hastings was arranged on the same day as his mother's funeral in Daylesford. Warren was baptised at Churchill by Nathaniel Sturges, who recorded in the parish register: 'Warren Son of the Revd Mr Penniston Hastings was baptiz'd'. Three days earlier, Nathaniel Sturges had buried the infant daughter of Joseph and Mary Ellis of Churchill, and Mary Ellis was therefore the obvious choice as wet-nurse and foster-mother to the infant Warren Hastings. His earliest days were therefore spent in the crowded home of Joseph Ellis, an agricultural worker with a family of his own. It was presumably to this period in his life that Warren Hastings was referring when he said of his childhood: 'I was then literally dependent upon those whose condition scarcely raised them above the level of absolute want.' Later in his life, Warren Hastings heard that his foster-mother had been left a widow and was receiving poor relief from the parish at two shillings and sixpence a week; by that time, of course, he was wealthy enough to ensure that adequate provision was made for her. His foster-brothers, too, took advantage of his well-known generosity by reminding him that they had been playmates together and 'had sucked at the same breast'. They, too, were not rejected.

Warren Hastings's father abandoned his two infant children soon after their mother's death, remarried, and emigrated to Barbados where he spent the rest of his life in comfort as Rector of Christ Church, a parish of slaves and sugar-cane. It was only through the good offices of her brother that Hester Warren's small inheritance in Cheltenham was secured to Warren Hastings. Warren and Anne Hastings spent their childhood years in the Churchill home of their grandfather, a hapless spendthrift who lived in a world of antiquarian unreality. Sixty years later, when he revisited the scenes of his childhood, Warren Hastings remarked that his grandfather's house was 'once a good house and still is in decent condition'. Nevertheless, the Vicar of Churchill was unimpressed by the alleged antiquity of the Hastings family, and probably regarded them with professional disapproval.

When he was about five years old, Warren Hastings began to attend school in the village. Presumably this was Lady Harcourt's School. Nathaniel Sturges implied that the education left much to be desired, but the children must have been taught to read and given basic instruction in numbers. Warren Hastings was an exceptionally bright pupil, and the extensive reading and writing that characterise the whole of Warren Hastings's adult life are an indication that his earliest education was not unduly defective. It was recorded (in 1841) that village labourers in Churchill recollected that 'Warren aye took his larning kindly', but little credence can be given to such remarks made more than a century later, and no doubt calculated to please the enquirer. However, Macaulay's statement that he 'learned his lessons on the same bench with the sons of the peasantry` is probably accurate'. Becoming acquainted with boys from the lower classes of society must have been a very valuable training for his work in India.

In 1737 Warren Hastings survived an attack of smallpox. In about 1738 or 1739 occurred the best-known incident in his childhood. He described this in a conversation with a friend more than sixty years later, and it was first made public in Gleig's Memoir of 1841. Warren Hastings was reported to have said:

> 'To lie beside the margin of that stream, and muse, was one of my favourite recreations; and there, one bright summer's day, when I was scarcely seven years old, I well remember that I first formed the determination to purchase back Daylesford.'

The incident is so inherently probable, corresponding both with Hastings's subsequent career and with his known character, that it may be accepted as genuine and autobiographical. Biographers, however, have speculated on the identity of the stream. Most probably he had wandered along the banks of the Evenlode until he reached Daylesford, or else perhaps he made his way down the hill from his grandfather's house to Churchill Mill, and that his favourite resort was by the nearby stream where his thoughts may perhaps have been turned to Daylesford by Thomas Andrews the miller, a Daylesford man himself. In his long years of exile, Warren Hastings never relinquished that ambition:

> The child's dream, as it did not appear unreasonable at the moment, so in after years it never faded away. God knows there were periods in my career when, to accomplish that, or any other object of honourable ambition, seemed to be impossible ... I can never express sufficient gratitude to the kind providence which permits me to pass the evening of a long, and I trust not a useless life, amid scenes that are endeared to me by so many personal as well as traditional associations

At the age of eight, Warren Hastings was removed from Churchill by his uncle Howard, a successful customs officer who became the two children's legal guardian after the death of their father in Barbados in 1744. No doubt his uncle thought it was high time the children were delivered from the ministrations of their grandfather. So far as we know, Warren Hastings did not return to his childhood home for forty-five years. In 1749 his guardian died, and he passed into the care of an even more distant relative, Joseph Creswicke of Moreton-in-Marsh, who nominated him as a writer in the East India Company service. This promised a good education and an honourable and lucrative career in India. The nomination led to the application for a baptismal certificate which was duly issued on 12<sup>th</sup> November 1749 by Nathaniel Sturges who was still the Minister of Churchill. A few weeks later, Warren Hastings, aged seventeen, set sail for Bengal.

It is not part of the story of Churchill to describe Warren Hastings's career in the East India Company. He was diligent, determined and reliable and in 1772 he was appointed Governor of Bengal. By 1774 his authority as Governor-General was extended over all the British territories in India. Ten years later, Warren Hastings left India, having laid the foundations of the future empire. Inevitably, he made enemies. He frequently acted in an arbitrary and autocratic manner, and his return to England was the signal for his impeachment and trial by the House Lords for serious irregularities in his administration, and particularly in his treatment of certain prominent Indian individuals. He was unfortunate in being made a pawn in an unseemly political dispute between the rival Whig and Tory parties. The trial, which lasted – on and off – for over seven years, consumed his immense private fortune and left him a dignified provincial recluse. He was never awarded the honour of at least a knighthood to which he was so justly due. But he married – twice – and spent his latter years in the company of his beloved wife, Anna-Maria.

He fulfilled his childhood dream in 1788 by buying Daylesford House which he rebuilt to his own taste and in a style reminiscent of his Indian days. By 1808 he had completed the purchase of all the freehold estates in Daylesford parish, including the patronage of his grandfather's church which he rebuilt in 1816, and had turned a detached island of Worcestershire into a minute Indian princedom. He died there on 22<sup>nd</sup> August 1818.

# ENCLOSURE

After the death of Sir Robert Walter in 1731, the Sarsden estate was inherited through his sister, Isabella Charlotte Walter, who had married John Rolle of Stevenstone, Devon. John Rolle had died in 1730, and so the estate passed to their son, another John Rolle (1712-1779), who, in accordance with Sir Robert's will, briefly changed his name to 'Walter` before reverting to his family name. The Rolles were a family of importance in Devonshire where John Rolle was their Member of Parliament. So far as we know, he made little more than the occasional visit to his Oxfordshire estate that was run by his steward, George Bulley, who may also have occupied Sarsden House.

In 1784, Denys Rolle, who had inherited Sarsden and Churchill from his brother John in 1779, put the whole estate up for sale, including in the advertisement the 'Rectory of Sarsden: present Rector near 70 years'. The implication of this curious (and inaccurate) information was that a prospective purchaser of the estate would also secure the advowson, and could shortly expect to be in a position to present a new rector to the parish – a living which had become more desirable as a result of the increased productivity of agriculture – and in consequence of the great tithes – during the eighteenth century. The Rector of Sarsden was still the Revd Tilleman Hodgkinson, aged 56, Prebendary of Llandaff; he died on 28th May 1786.

The death of Tilleman Hodgkinson enabled Denys Rolle to appoint a new Rector of Sarsden who was also the last to describe himself formally as Lecturer of Churchill. This was the Revd Arthur Saunder, aged forty-six, from South Molton in Devon, and presumably known personally to the Rolle family. Arthur Saunder had for many years been Vicar of Sidmouth (Devon) and seems to have been reluctant to move to Oxfordshire, for he was inducted as rector on 4<sup>th</sup> November 1786, resigned on 10th February 1787 and was then reinstated on 5<sup>th</sup> March 1787, being nominated Lecturer of Churchill three weeks later.

It is possible that Denys Rolle had failed to find a purchaser because the Sarsden estate was 'unimproved', that is to say, it had not been modernised by an Enclosure Act. His next move, therefore, was to proceed with the enclosure of the parishes of Sarsden and Churchill and the 'tything' (hamlet) of Lyneham, which was authorised by a Private Act of Parliament in 1787. The Enclosure Award was completed on 25<sup>th</sup> June 1788.

The cultivation of the open fields of Churchill had changed little since the Middle Ages. The arable land consisted of four great open fields, now divided into seven 'quarters', centred upon the village of Churchill from whence radiated a pattern of fieldways leading to every corner of the parish. The seven Quarters form four distinct groups:

|  | Acres | Roods | Perches |
|---|---|---|---|
| Cott Field (south and west of the village) | 441 | 1 | 18 |
| Swailsford and Ramswell (north) | 365 | 0 | 28 |
| Fittixmore and Hensdon (east) | 413 | 3 | 38 |
| Quar Hill and Woodside (north-east) | 366 | 3 | 14 |

These fields were cultivated in accordance with ancient parish custom on a rotation that allowed cereal crops to alternate with beans and pease and with a fallow year during which the field was restored and manured by the pasturing of animals. The seven-year rotation seems to have been: wheat – pease – barley or oats – fallow – wheat – barley – fallow. Each of these great open fields was divided into several hundred ridges – long narrow strips, each belonging to a different landowner. These strips were roughly 220 yards long by 22 yards wide, giving an area of 4840 square yards or one acre, the area that could traditionally be ploughed by one plough-team in one day. In reality, the ridges were often indeterminate in size, and on heavy clay soil might well be as little as eleven yards wide, or half an acre in area. The ridges were grouped into furlongs that consisted of about thirty acres, whose shape and position were determined by the local lie of the land. Every furlong had its own name, sometimes from the mists of time, and mostly now irretrievably lost. Neither the ridges nor the furlongs had any visible wall or hedge to act as a boundary, although, after centuries of ploughing, there was a tendency for a mound to develop along the length of each strip, and these mounds were used for access by foot when necessary. The absence of walls and hedges provided employment for the younger boys of the village as bird-scarers (from the crops) or to prevent sheep and cattle straying into the cultivated fields (Little Boy Blue). Furlongs (not to be confused with the linear measurement of 220 yards) were accessed by the field tracks along which plough teams, wagons and horses could be drawn as needed.

Originally it seems that the ridges were methodically distributed but were cultivated by the peasants (villeins) each of whom held about thirty, conventionally called a 'yardland'. This ensured that the villeins shared equally in good and poor soil, and in accessibility. But over the years slow changes had taken place. Wealthier peasants, by purchase, inheritance or exchange, built up larger holdings until they were obliged to lease some or all of their land to tenants. At the same time, they made an effort to group their ridges into more compact holdings. By the eighteenth century, these peasant landowners had become known as 'yeomen' or 'husbandmen' – there was no real distinction between the words – whereas peasants who rented land became known as farmers. In practice, many yeomen both cultivated their own land and also rented land from others. In legal theory, all the land except what was held freehold still belonged to the Lord of the Manor, and all the yeomen held their land only by virtue of their owning a copy or extract from the Custom Roll of the Manor, so they were called 'copyholders`. The agriculture was managed by a group of Fieldsmen chosen from the wealthier yeomen, but in every respect ancestral custom dictated where and what crops should be grown, and when the fields should be sown, harvested and turned to grazing. An admirable list of the names of all the quarters and furlongs in Churchill towards the end of the eighteenth century was drawn up by Arthur W. Ward and printed by Mrs Lilian Rose.[17]

---

17  *The History of Churchill*, pp 52-56.

Alongside the cultivated fields there were also meadows beside the streams that were particularly suitable for grazing by cattle and horses. These were held collectively, each copyholder being permitted to graze a fixed number ('stint') of animals in proportion to the area or number of yardlands in his arable landholding. Further away, on the hillsides and on poorer soil, there were the commons, used for sheep, rough grazing, and for the supply of stone and firewood. They were called 'commons', not because they were common land in the sense that we understand it today, but because the copyholders shared them in common, following the instructions of the fieldsmen and the ancient customs of the village. The cattle and sheep grazed together indiscriminately, although serious efforts were now being taken to ensure that the annual 'bulling' of the cows followed the principles of selective breeding. All the yeomen and husbandmen lived in homesteads in the village: there were no isolated 'farmhouses'. Those villagers who were not copyholders and owned no land of their own had, over the years, become landless agricultural labourers, and by the end of the eighteenth century they constituted by far the largest section of the village population.

To us today, this system seems unnecessarily complex and inefficient, as indeed it was to a certain extent. But over the years the yeomen had evolved strategies to make their work less strenuous and more productive. Even so, the system was labour-intensive and needed a radical overhaul. This was known as 'enclosure' and constituted a completely new pattern of landownership and farming. Enclosure appealed most to the lord of the manor, who stood to gain by the acquisition of what formerly had been regarded as waste land. But other village landowners welcomed a system whereby their land was consolidated in a compact area that made farming easier and permitted them to experiment with new crops, new rotations and scientific breeding of animals. At first, in the seventeenth century, enclosure had taken place by agreement amongst these landowners, sometimes not even formally documented. But by the 1780s, it was normal for a private agreement to enclose to be regulated by an accurate assessment of the land involved, followed by a Private Act of Parliament: one for each parish.

When Denys Rolle withdrew the advertised sale of the Sarsden estate, he proceeded at once with a plan to enclose Sarsden, Churchill and Lyneham that would make the estate a more attractive prospect for a potential buyer. This was authorised by a Private Act of Parliament in 1787, which appointed experienced commissioners who commissioned a professional survey of all the thousands of small parcels of land, each of which had to be identified by its size, land use, owner and by the name of the occupier who cultivated it. In Churchill alone there were 2842 separate acres. The survey was undertaken by Edward Webb of Stow-on-the-Wold, a highly respected professional land valuer, who employed the young William Smith, the future geologist, as his assistant in the process. The survey was completed very quickly, no doubt because of the inside knowledge of William Smith, and on 25th June 1788 the Enclosure Award, together with a detailed map and schedule, was publicised in the parish. This was a rapid process, as enclosure frequently took several years. But in Churchill there was only one main landowner, and therefore any objections to enclosure could be overruled – and the fact that Rolle needed an Act of Parliament indicates that there must have been at least one objection.

Normally, there is no record of the negotiation and bargaining that took place before the award was made, but the landowners tried to reach agreement amongst themselves so that the Enclosure Commissioners could at least have a shrewd idea of what new distribution they were expected to achieve. Some small yeoman farmers might even have decided that they could not afford the cost of the legal fees, let alone the hedging, ditching and road-building required, and so opted out by selling up to one of the greater landowners and becoming tenant farmers. Such arrangements do not appear in the wording of the Enclosure Award. However, in the case of Churchill, we have a fascinating and probably unique document. On the blank endpapers of a copy of the Enclosure Award for Oddington, Glos., held in the Gloucester County Record Office, someone has written a lampoon of the process of the Churchill enclosure, in the style of the Old Testament. There is no indication as to who wrote this, but clearly he was very well acquainted with undesirable aspects of the process. The book in which this was written appears to have belonged to John Hughes (born in 1748) who seems to have lived in Churchill, but John Hughes was neither a freeholder nor a tenant farmer, and it is hard to see how he could have known so much about the enclosure process. From the wording of the document itself, the finger points at Charles Tahourdin, Rector of Cornwell and Vicar of Churchill. The document is of such intrinsic interest that it is worth printing here, with a few explanatory comments.

## Chronicle of the Churchill Inclosure
## Chronicle of the Acts of Rollo the Elder and his Servant Bully

1    *And it came to pass that the wealthy Waterses died, & was buried, and was succeeded in possessions, that be near unto the Forest called Whichwood, by a certain wanderer called* Rollo *[Dennis Rolle alias Walter]*

2    *Now* Rollo *by his meanness & Tyranny, caused the people to hate him, inasmuch that his name waxed odious; for his Predecessor chastised them with whips, but he chastised them with scorpions.*

3    *He made a man of infamous Character a Ruler over the Husbandmen, and exalted the drunkard and blasphemer.*

4    *The Widow and Fatherless he deprived of their rights, by his oppression, and he discarded the man who grew Gray in his Service.*

5    *Now the Chieftain whom* Rollo *appointed over the people was of the Tribe of Lawyers, by some called Pettifoggers, a Man ignorant of his Profession, but of some low cunning, he was familiar with vice & a stranger to Virtue; and his name was called* Bully. *[George Bulley of Chadlington, a land agent]*

6    *And his well-beloved servant* Bully, *having his own Interest in view, spake unto his master saying, be it known unto thee, great* Rollo, *at all times and seasons, I will do you service; and as thou knowest I have no Character to lose, nothing but dread of hanging shall stop my career.*

7    For the advancement of my wealth we will apply to the Senate of the Nation [Parliament] and thy Lands shall be inclosed, the Commissioners shall be chosen from among thy dependants and the Man of the Chair shall be thy friend [The Chairman of the Churchill Enclosure Commissioners was the Revd John Davis of Bloxham. Others were Richard Richardson of Devizes and Francis Webb of Salisbury, Wilts.]

8    Young *Rollo* [John Rolle of Stevenstone, 1751-1842, Knight of the Shire for the County of Devon] is thy son, & heir, he is a man of much Impudence, and in bonds of friendship with the immaculate Minister [William Pitt the Younger, Prime Minister]; he will assist our cause and carry our Petition with a high hand, even until it receives the sanction of Royalty [George III].

9    Moreover should thy insignificant neighbours Demurr, I have procured Evidence, men who will speak as thou orderest before the representatives of the people [the House of Commons]; thy wine shall stir the evil spirit within them, and the hopes of obtaining thy favour shall make them utter false things.

10   Thus spoke his trusty servant *Bully;* and *Rollo* fell on his neck and kissed him, & said, blessed art thou among the Lawyers; the words of thy mouth are as sweet as honey to my soul, & a precious balm to my troubled mind, yea my weak body leapeth for joy.

11   Thy name fitteth thee well, Thou surely hast been edicated in the Schools of iniquity, for an honest man never spoke as thou Speakest; go therefore Conveane the people and may thy guardian Imp protect thee.

12   Then Bully went out from the presence of his Master, and caused a proclamation to be made in the weekly journal, and the people assembled together & wanted a Commissioner to act for them. [A notice was placed in Jackson's Oxford Journal for a meeting to be held at the Crown & Cushion Inn at Chipping Norton on 23rd January 1787 to discuss a bill to enclose Sarsden, Churchill, Lyneham, Merriscourt and Finescourt.]

13    *But Bully denied their request, and said, the Commissioners shall be whom my Master pleases; They then cried give us a Commissioner to protect our property, or peradventure Justice may not be done us.*

14    *But Bully still deaf to their Call of Justice became passionate [lost his temper] and swore and scoffed at them; when lo! A Man who owned the possessions usually pertaining to the Sons of Levy arose and called Bully a blackguard and scoundrel, which language frightened him sore.* [This must be the impropriator of the Great Tithes of Churchill, the Lay Rector, Lock Rollinson. Lock Rollinson is named in the Enclosure Act but he died in 1788 before the Award was made, and so the rectorial estate passed to his widow, Mrs Mary Rollinson. On 5th January 1788 Lock Rollinson put Churchill Rectory Farm on the market, around four hundred acres.]

15    *The meeting then broke up and every man returned to his own dwelling; Bully went home also, and prayed to the father of darkness for assistance.*

16    *He then went to the Great City* [London] *where the wicked are known to resort and there with the assistance of men of more ingenuity and power than himself, he forged the names of some to draw others into his snare.* [The other names in the Act are Robert Vansittart, Thomas Wood, and Dr Thomas Brookes, Vicar of Shipton-under-Wychwood]

17    *And they wot not what they did; for the veil of delusion was drawn before their faces.*

18    *And behold Men to bear witness were hurried up to the Great City, & they spake strange things before the senate, even such things as Rollo and his servant commanded, and they were rewarded with money. The owner of the tenths likewise received their cash & changed his tone.* [This is probably another way of referring to Lock Rollinson, although it could also apply to the Vicar of Churchill, the Revd Charles Tahourdin; if so, he can scarcely have been the author of this lampoon]

19    *Thus an Act passed bearing no date* [The Act is 27 George III c.27, 1787], *and* Rollo *and his servant obtained their ends, & every other persons Estate became unto him as no Estate at all, for it was at the disposal of the bosom friend of his Enemy.*

20    *Now the rest of the Acts of* Rollo *and his Champion, & all that they did; likewise the blustering tyranny of young* Rollo *(who made the people accept such Measures as pleased him) and all their other proceedings, are they not written in the remaining chapters of the Chronicles of the Churchill Inclosure.*

Well, no, unfortunately they were not. This scurrilous and libellous document was obviously not intended to be made public or taken seriously as an historical account, but it does suggest an accurate outline of events, and gives a flavour of the extreme bitterness which enclosures often provoked.

The effect of enclosure was dramatic, and was to be the most significant event in the modern history of the parish. In Churchill, fourteen farms were created within the Sarsden estate, each now leased to a tenant farmer. In addition there were several freehold properties that did not belong to the estate, but only one of these was a farm of any substantial size. The new farms each required a homestead or farmhouse. Some of the farmers continued to operate from their traditional home in the village, but others needed a new farmhouse at the centre of their compact integrated farms. The construction of these new farmhouses was quickly followed by the creation of new access roads to the farms. Farmland, that had previously consisted of several hundred ridges, was now enclosed into one farm, and the farmer was required to plant a quickset (hawthorn) hedge to separate his property from that of his neighbours. Within this farm, he then identified fields of arable, pasture and meadowland which rarely corresponded in situation to the old named furlongs of the open fields. A map showing all the field names in use in post-enclosure Churchill is printed in 'The History of Churchill' by Mrs Lilian Rose, at the beginning of this book.

After the enclosure award had been made, there were only four major landowners in the parish: the Sarsden Estate (Denys Rolle) at over 2,663 acres, Mrs Mary Rollinson (the Lay Rector, owning the tithes and the glebe land) at over 434 acres, and John Bulley Hacker, the Sarsden estate steward, who probably lived in Sarsden House, at over 115 acres. Arthur Saunder, in his capacity as Rector of Sarsden, was allotted a total of 191 acres in Sarsden and an annuity of £100 payable from Merriscourt Farms. In addition, of course, he held the Parsonage House in Sarsden for his life. By contrast, the Revd Charles Tahourdin, who as Vicar of Churchill had the real responsibility for the pastoral care of the parish, received a miserable fourteen acres in Swailsford Field, and the proceeds of an estate in Kingham purchased six years earlier. To supplement this, the Government had at some stage purchased for £200 two acres of land near Pershore that brought in an annual rent of £8. Altogether, the vicarage lands in Churchill produced a total stipend of about £80 a year.

In the Sarsden Estate were five hundred acres of former common land that now belonged to the Lord of the Manor. Of the remaining thirty-five freeholders, twenty-three owned very small areas – less than nine acres – and most of them were householders owning just their house and garden. These remaining Yeomen Farmers seem to have been Richard Gibbs (54 acres), Thomas Brookes (48 acres), Joseph Higgins (32 acres), Thomas Davis (25 acres), Joseph Harvey (21 acres), Elizabeth Hailes (18 acres), William Harvey (17 acres), Robert Brookes (16 acres), Alexander Betterton (16 acres), Richard Gilkes (15 acres), Thomas Watts (9 acres) and William Smith senior (9 acres). There were fourteen tenant farmers of the Sarsden Estate in Churchill, several of whom were renting very extensive farms. The Sarsden Estate kept 131 acres in hand, farmed directly from Sarsden. The fourteen farmers were Henry Colborn (388 acres), Thomas Smith (235 acres), Richard Rowland (168 acres), William Jacksons (158 acres), Robert Smith (151 acres), Thomas Boulter (146 acres), Thomas Brooks (84 acres), William Beman (67 acres), Thomas Roberts (65 acres), John Boulter (32 acres), Thomas Wright (18 acres), Thomas Andrews (6 acres), Thomas Davis (1 acre) and Giles Wallington (barely half an acre). The last four, although technically tenant farmers, did not occupy enough land to make a viable living from it. By combining yeomen and tenants, this gives a total of twenty-six farmers in Churchill by 1790.

The social consequences of Enclosure were that the class of tenant farmers increased at the expense of freeholding yeomen and husbandmen, and the class of copyholders virtually vanished. An increasing number of villagers now earned their living as agricultural labourers, working for the farmers on their new farms. There must still have been an almost invisible underclass of unemployable men, still dependent on outdoor parish relief, and this will have included all older men no longer fit to be employed. The disappearance of all former 'common' land meant that the underprivileged could no longer rely on its use for grazing, for firewood or for stone. But the concept of 'unemployment' had not yet arisen.

# WILLIAM SMITH

*William Smith*

*Reproduced by permission of the Geologicial Society of London*

The Enclosure Commissioners employed Edward Webb of Stow-on-the-Wold to undertake the survey of the parish. Every separate piece of land had to be measured, its agricultural use ascertained, and its owner and occupier identified. Since this was as yet an unenclosed village, the measurements included all the separate arable ridges that amounted to more than two thousand. This had then to be recorded on a precise and detailed map that would be used as the basis for the re-allocation of land between the new owners and occupiers. It is fair to say that the allocation was carried out with reasonable justice: but any former 'common' land was now held to belong to the manor. Edward Webb was a self-educated man who made all his own instruments – pentagraphs, theodolites, scales and compasses. Having arrived in Churchill, he needed the assistance of a capable and hard-working young man to hold the chain and make notes. He noticed that an eighteen-year old from the village was taking an intelligent interest in what Webb was doing, and, always anxious to encourage another self-educated surveyor, he asked him to talk about himself and his experience. The teenager – William Smith – explained that he had attended the village school, had taught himself the principles of surveying, and had had some practical experience working on his uncle's farm in Over Norton.

William Smith, who had been born in Churchill on 23$^{rd}$ March 1769, and baptised in the old church there on 9$^{th}$ April (probably by Edward Stone the Younger), was the eldest of five children of John and Ann Smith. His father, a blacksmith 'commonly known as "Hobbins", had been born in Kingham in 1735, but a few years later had been brought back to his family home in Churchill which consisted of a cottage and a smallholding of about ten acres. As there was another, well-established blacksmith in the village, John Smith seems to have specialised in making and mending the few pieces of machinery in use in a rural village – the mill-wheel and grindstones, the church bells, wagon wheels and the church clock. He had the reputation of being a 'very ingenious mechanic', but contracted pneumonia while erecting some machinery, and died in February 1777 leaving a widow and four young children. Two years later, his widow remarried to Robert Gardner from Long Compton – another Churchill man by birth – and the family continued to live in the ancestral home in Churchill, now long since demolished, but on a site adjacent to the former village school. Robert Gardner worked as a tailor, and shortly afterwards took up the licence for the Chequers Inn.

William Smith attended the village school in Churchill – Lady Harcourt's School – where he learnt to read and write and acquired the rudiments of arithmetic 'as far as the rule of three' – which is not very far! Later in life, he professed to despise his schooling. 'Grammar was not taught, nor do I recollect its ever being named, or one grammarian in the place, where vulgarisms in language and broad pronunciation were prevalent'. He was always self-conscious of his own deficiencies, yet William Smith had an astonishing intuitive intelligence that made him arguably one of the greatest natural scientists of his age.

He remained at school until he was eleven (1780), and, despite his misgivings, learned to write a fine copperplate hand, and was thoroughly grounded in arithmetic. On leaving school, he went to London for two years, arriving shortly after the notorious Gordon Riots. He retained vivid memories of his time in London, and was an alert and intelligent observer, seeing awful hangings on Tyburn's tree, terrible fires, and very probably encountering William Blake the artist who lived in the same district. On his return to Churchill in 1783, his father's brother, William, a farmer in Over Norton, took an avuncular interest in the thirteen-year old lad, encouraging him to take up surveying by providing him with books on geometry and mensuration, and involving him in the schemes of drainage and land improvement that were being undertaken as a result of the recent Chipping Norton Enclosure Act. William Smith responded enthusiastically, and applied himself with diligence to a process of self-education. He was therefore ideally equipped to become an assistant to Edward Webb when he came to begin the Churchill Enclosure in July 1787. It no doubt gave William Smith satisfaction to have his own name recorded on the final award as the owner of the smallest tithe-free freehold estate:

| | Acres | roods | perches | £ | s | d |
|---|---|---|---|---|---|---|
| Mr William Smith House and Garden Junior | 0 | 0 | 14 | 0 | 3 | 7¼ |
| Allotment in Heath Way | 0 | 2 | 39 | 0 | 14 | 0¼ |

His uncle, William Smith senior, was also listed:

| | Acres | roods | perches | £ | s | d |
|---|---|---|---|---|---|---|
| Allotment in Cottfield | 9 | 1 | 6 | 10 | 6 | 5 |

Altogether, the Smith inheritance amounted to just over ten acres, or, as William Smith calculated, five-eighths of a yardland.

William Smith's association with Edward Webb proved mutually satisfactory. *'I admired the talent of my master, his placid and unruffled temperament, and his willingness to let me get on, for I required no teaching.'* Edward Webb was soon able to entrust responsible work to his assistant and as early as 1788 Smith began to traverse the country on foot, covering prodigious distances, with a keen sense of direction and topography. During these long walks, William Smith's awareness of different soil and rock formations began to crystallise into a theory of stratification. In 1793, he applied these ideas to a detailed study of the coal-bearing strata at High Littleton, Somerset. From 1794 to 1799, while still in his twenties, he surveyed and superintended the construction of the Somerset Coal Canal. Ever since childhood, when he had been fascinated by the 'pundibs' and 'poundstones' of his native village, he had collected and studied fossils; he now formulated the theory that related the classification of fossils to the rocks in which they are found, and thus began the identification of the geological sequence of strata.

From 1800, William Smith became well-known as a Civil Engineer responsible for schemes of land-drainage and irrigation for landowners such as Thomas Coke of Holkham and the Duke of Bedford; conducting extensive reclamation in Norfolk and Suffolk; advising on canals such as the Kennet and Avon, and prospecting for coal in the Forest of Dean. But his main preoccupation was producing a series of detailed geological maps, drawn with increasing precision on the outline map of England produced by Cary, for which he is rightly regarded as the Father of English Geology.

Always conscious of his inadequate education, William Smith found difficulty in expressing himself coherently in writing. Moreover, he was a perfectionist, constantly planning a major publication, but failing to complete his self-set task. He was proud of his ancestors as freeholders and yeomen of Churchill, and it was only in great extremity that in 1808 he sold his own patrimony for £700. Financial difficulties were not his only problem: shortly after marriage his wife became insane in York Asylum. There were no children.

From the diaries and accounts that he kept intermittently throughout his life, we have a record of his occasional return visits to Churchill. In 1789 he was 'drawing the streets, freeholds &c of Churchill Town on another plan of the Great Lot.' In April 1802 and in September 1803 he paid brief visits to his home village where his younger brother Daniel was quietly prospering as a tailor. His uncle William died in 1805, and his mother in 1807.

The Smith family faced a crisis in 1808. William Smith's sister, Elizabeth, had married an excise officer, John Phillips, in 1798, and they had had four children. John Phillips died in January 1808, so Daniel Smith the tailor invited his widowed sister to bring her family back to Churchill.

However, Elizabeth Phillips herself died in Churchill in July 1808, leaving three children aged 8, 5 and 2, with their uncle Daniel. William Smith came to Churchill for a brief visit in September, bought six pairs of stockings from Brother Daniel, and together they examined the family accounts. William had already borrowed £50 from Daniel.

In December 1808 William Smith again came back to Churchill, and sold his ancestral home and smallholding to his step-father, Robert Gardner, using the proceeds to settle his debts. The account entered on 31st December 1808 is endorsed *N. B. These payments out of money received on* <u>*sale*</u> *of my* <u>*Land at Churchill*</u>. The payments consisted of

|  | £ | s | d |
|---|---|---|---|
| *paid Br[other] D[aniel] S[mith] note and Int[erest]* | 50 | 12 | 6 |
| *paid Shop Bill and int[erest]* | 66 | 14 | 0 |
| *paid bill for Br[other] J[ohn] S[mith]* | 34 | 5 | 0 |
| *paid J[ohn] Smith's Int[erest] to Ms*   50s 0d } | | | |
| *paid G Smith's Int[erest] to Ms*   30s 0d } | 4 | 0 | 0 |

The following day, William Smith took his nephew John Phillips and niece Ann Phillips by post-chaise from Churchill to Charterhouse Hinton in Somerset, leaving two-year old Jenkin Phillips with his uncle Daniel. William Smith adopted his nephew John, training him as his assistant, and instructing him in geology. Later, Professor John Phillips became a geologist in his own right, and the biographer of his uncle, William Smith.

Ten years elapsed before William Smith next returned to Churchill. This time, he came for two months, staying with Brother Daniel and meeting old friends such as Edward Webb. He arrived on 14th November 1818 in time to enjoy the merriment of the Churchill Wake week 'to which, among other idlers, the gypsies still gathered from the "Forest" of Whichwood', and then contacted J. H. Langston, the Squire of Sarsden who had invited him. The two men – James Langston in his early twenties, rich and ambitious, and William Smith, humble but erudite, now approaching fifty – walked the Sarsden Estate together, while

Langston sought advice and Smith recalled his childhood. Langston commissioned William Smith to irrigate his meadow alongside the Sars Brook – not a major undertaking in comparison with William Smith's usual work, but one which must have given him particular satisfaction. In his diary he recalls the day-to-day progress of the works:

*24 Nov 1818* Wet m[orning] Afterwards with Mr James Brooks ploughing out works of water mead. [A year later, James Brooks married Daniel Smith's daughter, Elizabeth.]

*25 Nov* Setting out marks at Watermead and instructing men. Formed dam and got water out.

*26 Nov* Got Trunk laid in W[ater] Mead

*28 Nov* Went to Mead with Steward and with Mr Hodges to Shultenham & took levels for watering it. [Shultenham Lot Meadow lay alongside the Evenlode on Churchill Heath Farm.]

*30 Nov* At Levels for Pond head Mr B[rooks]'s Water Meadow and setting out W[ater] Mead.

*1 Dec* At Br[other] Dan[ie]l's drawing up report on Pond and Water meadows for Mr Langston.

*2 Dec* M[orning] walked to Sarsden great House with Plan and Report.

*4 Dec* M[orning] walked to Sarsden & back to Churchill by W[ater} Mead

*5 Dec* M[orning] went to Mr Brooks' W[ater] M[ead} and directed works

*8 Dec* Butler came with message from Farmer Freeman

*9 Dec* Walked to Mr Atkins's [the steward of the Sarsden Estate] and to B[rooks]'s & Freeman's meadows

William Smith completed the assignment in less than three weeks, but he stayed in Churchill until 15th December, and found time for recreation: he was delighted to find the gravestones of his great-grandparents in Idbury churchyard (although he was disappointed that they did not prove that he was descended from Sir Walter Raleigh); he walked to Stow Sports Day with Edward Webb; he attended the Bolter's christening, and took tea at Sarsden with J. H. Langston's steward. His nephew, John Phillips, later recorded that it was on this occasion that William Smith collected 'marlstone' fossils from an excavation at Churchill Mill, and noted in detail the changes that had occurred since he left the village thirty years before. *'One of the largest and most honoured elms had fallen; the great common field was but a name … and Mr Smith yet found among the old inhabitants some who could remember the digging of Sarsden Pond, with its "golden" stones (iron pyrites), and the ornamental planting of Daylesford by "Governor Hastings", and laugh with him over the marvellous tales of "horses having run their feet off" in dragging the "fly coaches on the Oxford Road".'*[18]

William Smith made a brief visit to Churchill accompanied by his nephew John Phillips to celebrate the New Year 1820 with his brother Daniel. From then onwards he lived in the north of England, increasingly afflicted by rheumatism and deafness. In 1831 he was the first to be awarded the Wollaston Medal by the Geological Society of London 'in consideration of his being a great original discoverer in English Geology; and especially for his having been the first, in this country, to discover and teach the identification of strata, and to determine their succession by means of their embedded fossils'. Recognition had come at last. In 1835 he was created an honorary Doctor of Law of Trinity College, Dublin.

On his way to the British Association meeting in Birmingham, he stayed a few days at Churchill and visited some of his old friends. Taken ill at Northampton, he died there on 28th August 1839, aged 70. In 1891 the Earl of Ducie erected a memorial in Churchill to the memory of

---

18  John Phillips: Memoirs of William Smith Ll.D.,.1844, new edition 2003, passim.& pp 90 – 91.

William Smith, consisting of a monolith standing on a double base. The monument is formed of huge Oolitic stones from the district – the name 'Oolite` having been given by William Smith to the rocks that form the higher grounds in the locality.

William Smith's discoveries became a major landmark in science's challenge to traditional religious ideas, and together with Darwin's theory of evolution placed a massive question mark against the accepted belief that the universe was created in 4004 B.C. Yet Smith himself was probably unaware of the implications of his work. He accepted implicitly the activity of God the Creator, forming the earth 'according to regular and immutable laws, which are discoverable by human industry and observation.' Each stratum, together with its associated life-forms, must have been a separate creation following a divinely ordained plan. William Smith seems unaware of any conflict between his geology and the Genesis story. Perhaps Bible teaching was neglected in his childhood; perhaps William Smith quietly compartmentalised his science and his religion. We shall never know, for he was above all an intensely private person. He subscribed to the religious conventions of his day; with the wages that he received from Edward Webb he bought himself a Prayer Book, and he made an effort to be home in Churchill for Easter. But he took care not to disclose any evidence of personal faith, just as his diary, with its daily entries, made no reference to intimate events such as his mother's death and his own marriage, and private matters were recorded in an indecipherable code. Having surveyed the battle-field, William Smith left it to others to fight the war.

# JAMES HAUGHTON LANGSTON

After enclosure, the Sarsden estate was sold in 1792 to James Haughton Langston, a wealthy London wine merchant and founder of the banking firm of Langston, Twogood and Amory. He was said 'to be worth one million sterling'. He died three years later and was succeeded by his son, John Langston, Director of Sun Life Insurance, Member of Parliament and one of the Directors of the Bank of England. John Langston was Sheriff of Oxfordshire 1804-5, but died after a long illness on 11th February 1812. The arrival of the Langstons in the Sarsden Estate and Churchill village heralded important changes in the social and economic pattern of the district.

*James Haughton Langston of Sarsden (1796-1863), MP c.1840*

John Langston's son, James Haughton Langston (1796-1863) was a sixteen-year old schoolboy at Eton when his father died in 1812. He matriculated at Christ Church, Oxford, two years later, but did not complete an academic course, although he received an honorary D.C.L. in 1819[19].

Throughout his life, James Haughton Langston normally lived at Sarsden House, and took a personal interest in the estate. In 1820 he was elected one of the two Members of Parliament who represented the parliamentary borough of Woodstock, being then aged 24. Woodstock

---

19  Christine Peters, *The Lord Lieutenants and High Sheriffs of Oxfordshire,* 1995.

was in the 'pocket` of the Duke of Marlborough who sponsored Tory candidates. At the next election, Langston stood as a reforming Whig, while the Duke put up two Tories for election. Langston was defeated by only eight votes from a total electorate of 134. However, in the same election Langston also stood as a Whig candidate for the City of Oxford, topping the poll there with 1054 votes, and continued to represent Oxford as a Whig until 1835, again from 1841 to 1846, and then as a Liberal from 1847 to 1857 and from 1859 until his death in 1863, a total of over thirty-five years in parliament. In addition to his political career, Langston was Master of the Heythrop Hunt, Verderer of Wychwood Forest and a well-known progressive agricultural landowner and patron of architecture. In 1825 he had Sarsden House extensively remodelled by G.S.Repton. During his life, many of the farmhouses on his estate were built or rebuilt, and he took a leading part in providing Chipping Norton with a Town Hall (G.S.Repton, 1844), and Milton-under-Wychwood with a church and school (G.E.Street, 1854). He helped to promote the branch railway from Kingham to Chipping Norton (1854) by providing the required land at little more than its agricultural value. In view of his long political career, his reforming sympathies, his wealth and aristocratic connections, and his influential position in Oxfordshire, it is curious that Langston never received as much as a knighthood from the Whig and Liberal ministries that he supported.

*Sarsden House, ca 1910*

It seems possible that the project to build a substantial new church at Churchill may have begun to take shape in 1817 to commemorate his coming of age. If so, other projects crowded in, and the new Churchill Church was temporarily set aside. In 1823 Langston employed G.S.Repton to design a cruciform extension to St James's Church, Sarsden, providing transepts and a chancel.

The project to build a new church at Churchill must be seen as part of the overall transformation of the Sarsden Estate by an outstanding improving landlord of the nineteenth century. By 1825 the project was resumed. On 26th March 1825, Edward Legge, Bishop of Oxford, granted a faculty for the demolition of the old church. Skelton's picture of the old church in 1826 was made during the demolition and is therefore not evidence of any severe dilapidation. In the picture, the south aisle has lost its roof, and much of the tower is gone, but sufficient is still standing for us to realise that the medieval church in Churchill had been attractive and substantial, and its demolition was an act of brash vandalism that would not have been permitted by a later generation. There is no record of the fate of the interior furnishings, the stained-glass windows with the arms of the de Nowers and of Richard, Earl of Cornwall, the delicate curvilinear tracery, the pulpit and pews, the font, as well as the great Bible and Prayer Book provided in 1720. We can, however, quickly dispose of one myth: experts are convinced that the Sarsden Butter Cross does not embody the font from the old Churchill church. Doubtless there were many parishioners who were saddened to see their familiar and venerable church wantonly destroyed at the whim of a wealthy young man, but if so there is no recorded protest, which is not surprising when it is remembered that tenancies and livelihoods were dependent upon the same landlord. Only the chancel of the old church was retained, containing a handful of the former twenty-three memorials, to be used as a mortuary chapel and now as the Churchill Heritage Centre. It seems likely that the stone fabric of the old church that was not re-used in the construction of the new was conveyed to the foot of the hill where major construction work was being done on the site of Churchill mill. Mrs L. Rose[20] says that during renovations of

---

20  op.sit. p.29.

the water mill in 1933 the builders found pieces of masonry that may have belonged to the old church at Churchill. In 1985, Mr Alan Catling, while converting his barn into a dwelling, uncovered several pieces of carved stonework that evidently came from the old church. On 3rd May 1825 the Bishop licensed a barn belonging to J. H. Langston, previously used by Mr Taylor, a farmer, in which services could be held while the new church at Churchill was being built, implying that at least some of the fabric of the old church was to be incorporated in the new.

The site selected for the new church, on part of a field called the Home Ground (rented by Mr Phillips of Kingham) was most appropriate, not only being central and prominent in the life of the village, but also embodying the very name of the parish. For this work, Langston did not employ G. S. Repton, but chose to engage an Oxford architect, John Plowman, to design the new church that meets with short shrift from Miss Jennifer Sherwood[21] who describes it as 'the usual Georgian preaching box'. Certainly, the style is unashamedly derivative: the tower is a two-thirds scale replica of the Perpendicular tower of Magdalen College, Oxford, and the hammerbeam roof of the nave is patterned on Christ Church hall. The buttresses, surmounted by crocketed pinnacles, bear a resemblance to those on New College chapel. A notable feature, derived from the Magdalen College tower, is the external staircase leading to the ringers' chamber, with its associated outside pulpit. The stone tracery is in a different style in each window. But the church lacks the solidity of a genuine medieval building, and, although it is well-suited to musical concerts, those who preach here are well aware that the acoustics are unhelpful.

The church was built with local stone, but the pulpit and font are of Caen stone, and the pews are of polished oak with elm seating. Local masons were employed in the construction, and when the tower was completed, Mr Stokes, one of the masons, climbed to the top of one of the pinnacles and drank a stoup of ale to the health of all who had helped to build the church. Some of the bells from the old church were re-hung, and others were recast in 1826 from the original metal by

---

21  Pevsner's 'Oxfordshire', 1974, p.545.

Robert Taylor and Sons of Oxford, to form a peal of six. The old tenor bell, probably cast by James Keene in 1630, was inscribed:

*Our mournful sound doth warning give*
*That man cannot heare all wayes live.*

The clock, which contains some unusual and unique features, was also made by Robert Taylor of Oxford. Music was originally provided by a small orchestra accommodated as tradition required in the west end gallery, and accompanied by a large barrel organ. One of the drums of this organ is preserved in the Heritage Centre; it is curious that one of the tunes on this drum is named 'Sarsden', although sadly it can no longer be identified. Presumably the choir, for which Churchill was well-known, was seated in the choir stalls at the east end. A silver communion service of chalice, paten, paten on foot and tankard flagon, hallmarked 1826 by Paul Storr, was presented by J. H. Langston. A fine set of leather-bound Bibles and Prayer Books of the same year is preserved in the vestry. The wrought-ironwork on the inner doors of the church is discreetly stamped with the name of the local craftsman, 'W. Keen`.

The rebuilding was completed in 1826, but the new church was not consecrated for divine service until 1827, presumably owing to the death of Bishop Legge. In his place, Charles Lloyd of Christ Church, Regius Professor of Divinity, was enthroned on 4th March 1827. The consecration of All Saints Church at Churchill was then fixed for Saturday 20th October 1827, the Bishop travelling on to Burford afterwards to preach there the following day in support of the local Sunday School, and stopping on Monday to consecrate the new churchyard at Hailey on his way back to Oxford. Although no-one knew it at the time, the consecration took place on the same day as the Battle of Navarino[22], the major international event of the year. The new church retained the dedication to 'All Saints'.

---

22  The Battle was fought on 20th October 1827. To further their support of the Greeks in their War of Independence from the Ottoman Empire, the combined British, French and Russian fleets destroyed the Egyptian navy that was being used by the Turks, and thus guaranteed Greek independence.

Details of the consecration service have been preserved. The Rector of Sarsden, churchwardens and parishioners met the Bishop at the door and presented the Petition for Consecration. Then, led by the Rector, they processed to the Communion Table repeating the 24th Psalm responsively. The parishioners then took their seats, while the Bishop took up his position on the north side of the Communion Table. The sentence of consecration was read, signed by the Bishop, and laid on the Table. The Rector, the Revd Charles Barter (who was also of course the Vicar of Churchill) then conducted Morning Prayer, including the General Thanksgiving and a prayer led by the Bishop. The choir sang part of Psalm 26 before the Bishop began the service of Holy Communion. The Bishop's chaplain read the Epistle, the Rector read the Gospel, the Bishop led the Creed and the choir sang Psalm 100. Charles Barter preached the sermon. Finally, witnesses to the consecration signed their names to the document that was handed to the Bishop to be deposited in the diocesan archives.

# THE REVD CHARLES BARTER

*The Revd Charles Barter (1817-1868)*

Following the death of Arthur Saunder in 1816, J. H. Langston in his capacity as patron presented the Revd. Charles Barter to be the next Rector of Sarsden and Vicar of Churchill. Charles Barter was aged 31, and came from a family of Devonshire clergymen who for three generations had been educated at Balliol College, Oxford. Six months after his induction, on 21st November 1817, Charles Barter married Elizabeth Catherine Langston, the elder sister of his patron, J. H. Langston – an event almost certainly planned long before his institution in the living. A new and elegant Rectory House was specially commissioned from the architect, G. S. Repton, and in this house (now called 'Sarsden Glebe') Charles and Elizabeth Barter lived for fifty years and brought up their family of ten children, with the help of ten residential servants, in a style appropriate to the squire's brother-in-law. Two other sisters of J. H. Langston, Henrietta (1798-1844) and Julia (1806-1869) never married, but lived together in the nearby Sarsgrove House, also designed for them by G. S. Repton in 1825.

The main preoccupation during Barter's first decade as Rector was the building of the new church. Two years later, in 1829, Charles Barter received a dispensation from the Bishop of Oxford to allow him to be the Rector of Cornwell in plurality with his freehold of Sarsden and Churchill.

The association of these three parishes made sense geographically, and their estimated combined annual stipend (Cornwell £150, Sarsden and Churchill £510) provided a comfortable living and enabled Barter to employ a resident assistant curate to occupy the Rectory at Cornwell and to conduct morning prayer each Sunday at Churchill.

On 30th March 1851, despite much opposition from the Church of England and the open hostility of the Bishop of Oxford, the government carried out a census of church attendance. This revealed a massive increase in the number of dissenters nationally – especially Methodists – and an unsatisfactory level of attendance at many parish churches. The clergy were at pains to point out that the census was unreliable as the weather had been bad that day, and dissenters were suspected of inflating their numbers. In response to the disturbing results of the census, Bishop Samuel Wilberforce undertook an Episcopal Visitation of his diocese three years later, sending out a detailed questionnaire to each parish. By an Order in Council dated 17th July 1851, the benefice of Sarsden and the benefice of Churchill were united. This meant that the two parishes shared a single priest, and Charles Barter began the practice of referring to his benefice as 'Sarsden-cum-Churchill', but this had no legal authority and the parish of Churchill remained a separate vicarage until the union with Kingham and Daylesford one hundred and fifty years later. At the time of the 1854 Visitation, there was some confusion at diocesan level over the status of the parish of Churchill. The Bishop had originally addressed enquiries separately to the Rector of Sarsden and the Rector of Cornwell only, to which Charles Barter replied promptly, observing that he had not received an enquiry for the parish of Churchill. He then received a peremptorily worded note from the Bishop accusing him of not replying to two requests for information about Churchill, pointing out the inconvenience caused to the Bishop by such negligence, and requiring an immediate reply. Charles Barter, somewhat aggrieved, reminded the Bishop that this was the first enquiry that he had received for Churchill.

By comparing the ecclesiastical census return with the written replies that Charles Barter sent to the Bishop in 1854, we can form a reasonably accurate picture of Sunday worship in the parishes. Barter recorded that the 10.30 service of Morning Prayer at Churchill was conducted by the Curate of Cornwell – The Revd James Beck in 1851, followed by the Revd William Marah, licensed in June 1852. At this service the congregation numbered 96, with a further hundred Sunday School children. At the same time, Charles Barter was conducting a service of Morning Prayer for a congregation of sixty at Sarsden, the service being enriched by a choir of ten singing boys from Churchill School. There was also a separate service of Morning Prayer at Cornwell. At 3pm, Evening Prayer at Churchill was attended by a congregation from the whole benefice, and Charles Barter preached. Barter estimated that the average attendance at these services was normally slightly larger: one hundred each at Churchill and Sarsden, and 350 at the combined service in the afternoon. His curate at Cornwell, however, with disarming honesty, admitted that his attendance of 39 adults and 26 children was as many as he would have expected. In his return to Bishop Wilberforce's Visitation three years later, Barter estimated the average morning congregation at Churchill alone to be between 400 and 500, with rather more in the afternoon when parishioners from Sarsden attended. He pointed out that the capacity of Churchill church – free sittings for 500 – would scarcely permit of any further increase in the size of the afternoon service, although Morning Prayer, here and elsewhere in the neighbourhood, was less well-attended. The morning congregation at Sarsden numbered between seventy and ninety, depending on whether the Langston family was in residence: they were absent in Town for the census of 1851. These figures must be read with caution since by 1854 there was a dissenting chapel in Churchill attended by a congregation estimated by Barter at twenty. The total population of Churchill in 1851 was 645 and of Sarsden 188 plus the Langston household. If we accept Barter's figures, attendance at the Churchill parish church was approximately 64% of the population – well above the average of 48% calculated by Dr Kate Tiller for the county as a whole[23]. The sacrament of Holy Communion was celebrated eight times a year in Churchill and four times a year in Sarsden. There were about one hundred communicants in Churchill and forty to fifty in Sarsden.

---

23   ed. Kate Tiller, *Church and Chapel in Oxfordshire 1851*, ORS Vol. 55 1987.b

In addition there was an evening service in Churchill on Fridays during Lent at which Charles Barter gave a lecture.

Throughout his life, Charles Barter tended to be overshadowed by his better-known younger brother, Robert Speccott Barter, who was a Fellow of New College 1809-1832 and Warden of Winchester School from 1832 until his death in 1861. Amongst the stories of the legendary physical prowess of Warden Barter, there is one associated with Sarsden. Robert Barter set out to walk from Oxford to Sarsden, a distance he estimated to be eighteen miles. At Woodstock he overtook the carriage of the Bishop of Oxford.

"Where are you going?" called the Bishop.

"To Sarsden, my lord."

"I am going there too: can I give you a lift?"

"No thank you: I am rather in a hurry", Barter replied, and continued on his way on foot, arriving at Sarsden some time before the Bishop.

This incident throws light on the problems of travel before the development of railways locally in the 1850s. Robert Barter's name occurs frequently in the Churchill parish registers, reminding us that after the death of his father in 1846 Charles Barter, as head of the family, continued to provide in Sarsden Rectory a gathering place for his wide circle of friends and relations, who included his younger brother, William Brudenell Barter, Rector of Highclere and Burghclere; his son, Henry Barter, Vicar of Lamborne and later of Shipton-under-Wychwood; and his son-in-law, William E.D.Carter, also Vicar of Shipton-under-Wychwood until 1868.

Despite a personal friendship with John Keble, Charles Barter was a staunch churchman of what was sometimes described as 'the old school', and had his misgivings of the effect of the Oxford Movement. When the office of Rural Dean was revived in the Church of England in 1836, Charles Barter was appointed (1837) the Rural Dean of the newly-created Chipping Norton Deanery. In this capacity he consulted Bishop Samuel Wilberforce early in 1848 about one of the local clergy who was guilty of 'fraternizing with dissenters'. The Bishop fully shared Barter's prejudices, and in his reply (14th March 1848) agreed that the line that the unnamed clergyman had adopted made it impossible 'for you to ask the clergy to meet him at such discussions with any hope of profit', and instructed Barter not to invite him to the Clergy Chapter of the Deanery.

Intolerant and uncharitable attitudes such as these encouraged the growth and strength of institutional nonconformity. A few villagers from Churchill had joined Chipping Norton Baptist Church (founded 1775) and presumably walked to Chipping Norton for Sunday services. They included Ann Grimmet[t], John Box, William Grimmett, Mary Grimmett and others. John Box's dying words (1805) were recorded in the Baptist records: "I am going to rest in the arms of Christ". Primitive Methodists, who may have existed in Churchill since their licence of 1799, seem to have been accidentally omitted from the ecclesiastical census of 1851. But very shortly afterwards a Primitive Methodist Society had been formed in Churchill, and a Trust Deed for a chapel was drawn up on 17th December 1852. The building was erected during the next six months, since it is described in an indenture of mortgage dated 17th May 1853. This description refers to a piece of land in Churchill, 31 feet by 21 feet, belonging to the dwelling house of Thomas Gardner, in which had been erected a Chapel and Meeting House and School for the Primitive Methodist Connexion. The school, presumably, was a Sunday School but may have provided basic literacy in those days before universal education. The Trust Deed, which follows the standard pattern of such documents, lists twelve Trustees of whom six were local – three from Churchill and three from Lyneham. The three Churchill Trustees were John Margetts, labourer, who headed the list; William Hunt, baker, and Charles Peachey, labourer. Of the three, only Charles Peachey was literate. It is most probable that this is the chapel situated at the rear of Haughton House and long since disused. Charles Barter later described it as 'a very small Ranting or Primitive Methodist Chapel'. (Primitive Methodists were commonly called 'Ranters'). Thomas Gardner, on whose property it was built, was closely related to the Robert Gardner who had married William Smith's mother; he was a freeholder and smallholder, and must have been the Steward or leader of the little church. The property was mortgaged to John Gauthern of Sibford for £60 that was eventually paid off. John Gauthern was also one of the Trustees – the only one to be described as a 'gentleman'. The majority of members, like Margetts and Peachey, were agricultural labourers, and oral tradition tells us that the Sarsden Estate strongly disapproved of the Methodists and discriminated against them when they sought employment. In 1854 Charles Barter estimated the number of dissenters of all kinds in the parish at about twenty, but this is likely to be an underestimate and certainly will have excluded children[24].

*Interior of Old Methodist Chapel*

Although Charles Barter's four surviving sons (a fifth died in infancy) were sent away to Public Boarding School for their education, he was content for all his six daughters to attend the village school. The four boys all proceeded to Oxford University. A younger son, Henry,

---

24  I am grateful to the Revd Philip Poyner for allowing me to examine and transcribe some of the documents in the Chipping Norton Methodist Circuit Safe.

followed most closely in the family tradition by being ordained in 1858 and becoming Vicar of Shipton-under-Wychwood ten years later. He married Kate Moberly, the daughter of George Moberly, Headmaster of Winchester School where Robert Barter was the Warden. Charles Barter's daughter, Ellen, baptised in 1830 married William Edward Dickson Carter who was his father-in-law's Curate in Cornwell in 1846, and who was to succeed him as Rector of Sarsden and Rural Dean.

Samuel Wilberforce, the Bishop of Oxford, stayed with Charles Barter at Sarsden in March 1867, as the base for his projected Mission to Chipping Norton. On 14th March he accompanied the Rural Dean and his daughter to an early service of Holy Communion in Chipping Norton at which the Revd W.E.D.Carter preached 'an admirable sermon' on the tests on which the indwelling of Christ in the believer may be detected – a sense of awe, spiritual strength, and a desire to pray. After taking confirmation services at Milton-under-Wychwood and Leafield, the party drove back to Sarsden Rectory through heavy snowdrifts. On the following day (15th March) the Bishop held a confirmation at Churchill, and then consecrated the newly extended burial ground in Chipping Norton and addressed the employees from William Bliss's tweed mill. Despite the continuing bitterly cold weather, the Bishop, Archdeacon and Charles Barter visited Kingham the following afternoon for a confirmation there – 'altogether nicest this year' – and then, after dining at the White Hart, Bishop Wilberforce returned to Cuddesdon.

The Revd Charles Barter, Rector of 'Sarsden-cum-Churchill' and Cornwell and Rural Dean of Chipping Norton died on 24th June 1868. As a memorial to him, his widow, Elizabeth (1794-1878), sister of J.H.Langston, restored the chancel of the old church in 1869 as a mortuary chapel and for use at funerals. A lancet window, by C.C.Rolfe, was set in the blocked arch of the old Decorated east window. Inside, the little chancel was fitted with pine seats, and was provided with a new oak communion table, the original table having been transferred to the new church. The chancel arch (or perhaps the south doorway) was retained as a frame for the new west doorway, and perhaps now – or in 1826 – the bell turret was erected at the west end of the roof. Elizabeth Barter may have felt a sentimental attachment to the church where she must often have worshipped as a girl, and where her husband had conducted services for the first ten years of their married life; certainly, the little old chapel amongst the trees in the quiet graveyard has kept a warm place in the affection of the parishioners. It is fitting that it has now been beautifully restored and equipped as the Churchill Heritage Centre.

In 1827 Charles Barter recorded:

*Altho' it had long since been legally provided that no funerals should take place in the Burying Ground at Sarsden and the Burying Ground at Churchill should be common to both parishes, I found that notwithstanding it had been the practice to enter the burials of Sarsden in a separate Register Belonging to that parish, and I have continued to do the same.*

*I found likewise that a great number of the Parishioners of Sarsden had transferred their residence to Churchill, new cottages having been built there instead of at Sarsden as the old ones in the latter place fell into Decay, by John Langston Esq. and his son James Haughton Langston Esq. to whom almost the whole of both Parishes belong; – but that the Baptisms of such Parishioners of Sarsden as were in consequence of their residence at Churchill baptized in Churchill Church had notwithstanding been always entered in the Register of the Parish of Sarsden.*

The systematic depopulation of Sarsden may have started in 1795 when John Langston employed Humphrey Repton to landscape Sarsden Park. If so, there is little trace of any resettlement in Churchill in the census of 1851. The population of Sarsden continued to rise from 92 in 1801 to a peak of 188 in 1851, whereas Churchill reached its peak (665) as early as 1821. Churchill thus conformed to the general pattern of population growth only until 1821, but thereafter, for reasons not yet known, numbers declined, with a sharp dip at the time of the agricultural depression in 1881. This decline continued until, in 1931, the population had fallen below 430. By 1851 there was considerable immigration into the village from elsewhere: almost half the adult working population of

Churchill in 1851 originated outside the parish. There were also no less than twenty paupers living in Churchill, so the shifting insecurity of the population may explain the remark that 'none of the old families are left in Churchill'.

*Cottage at Sarsden*

In 1852, Gardner's Directory recorded that the two principal landowners in Churchill were the Revd Thomas Oakley and J.H.Langston. Thomas Oakley was Master of Charlbury Grammar School and curate there; he also served the cures of Leafield and Minster Lovell[25] Presumably he had acquired the rectorial tithes and glebe land of Churchill. Surprisingly, however, Langston was not Lord of the Manor: this honour belonged to Sir J(ohn) C(handos) Reade. W.H. Marah was curate in charge of Churchill under Charles Barter. There were seven farmers in the parish, as well as Jeremiah Beesley the schoolmaster, a grocer, a butcher, a baker, a blacksmith, a tailor, a miller, two shoemakers and Joseph Rose, licensed victualler at The Chequers. Not all the tradesmen would have had separate shops, but the grocer, the butcher, the smith and at least one shoemaker would have had their own premises.

---

25  Diana McClatchey: *Oxfordshire Clergy* 1777-1869, p.139.

# CHURCHILL MILL

In 1086 there were two mills in Churchill. One may have been by Standbow Bridge on the Evenlode and the other where the remains may still be seen at the foot of Hastings Hill. Every village needed a water-powered corn mill that normally belonged to the Lord of the Manor, but the particular skills required in operating the mill meant that the tenancy often remained in the same family for several generations. The last occasion on which I have traced a reference to 'Mills' in the plural is in the will of George Morecroft (1661) who apparently occupied the manor house, but it is probable that the mill on the Evenlode had fallen into disuse before the end of the medieval period.

The first identifiable miller of Churchill was Henry Chapman in c.1700, followed in c.1729 by Richard Baker. But during much of the eighteenth century, the miller of Churchill was Thomas Andrews (c.1710-1789) who also seems to have operated Daylesford mill. The footpath between the two was until recently called 'Miller's Path`. It may have been during his tenancy that the present mill buildings were erected. The mill is situated so far above the water level of the Swail Brook that a canal was constructed from further upstream to bring water to the mill where it could be collected in a millpond until there was sufficient head of water to power the massive water wheels. This canal or leet may still be seen as a shallow dry valley, and a weir and sluice-gate were constructed. Thomas Andrews was succeeded by his son, another Thomas (1738-1809). It was during their time that the young William Smith found his earliest fossils. Thomas Andrews was recorded as the miller in the Sarsden Terrier of 1790 which refers to the mill 'with the Messuage, Millpond and garden (three roods and three perches), the Lower Ham (three acres, one rood and seventeen perches) and the Upper Ham (one acre, three roods and thirty-two perches)'. The hams were the meadows between the mill and the stream, which the miller used for grazing. By the time that the estate had passed to the Langstons, significant alterations were taking place. Another detailed map of 1795 shows the mill now extended as a single building across the mill-stream, thus bringing the water-wheel inside the main structure. Beyond the mill, the road swung westwards to follow the line of 'Sandy Lane' towards Kingham. By 1818 the miller was Richard Edwards, and in the winter of 1818-1819 excavations were taking place at the mill – perhaps the mill-leet was being re-dug – and William Smith was delighted to revisit the site and collect some more marlstone fossils. Robert Plot, the seventeenth century natural historian of Oxfordshire, had remarked on the flock of pigeons that settled on a ground close to Churchill Mill on account of a saline spring there. In 1871, Professor John Phillips[26] listed seven parishes in Oxfordshire where 'sulphurous waters occur' and one of these is Churchill. In this case only, John Phillips gave a precise location: Churchill Mill. Is it too much to suggest that he obtained his information from his uncle, William Smith of Churchill? The saline or sulphurous spring near Churchill Mill has disappeared without trace.[27]

The period between the 1780s and the 1850s was a time of growth and prosperity for millers. There was a much increased grain production as a result of enclosure and the agrarian revolution, but the absence of a reliable road or rail system meant that much of this corn was still milled locally. Water-mills flourished in almost every parish in this area, even though they tended to be slow and inefficient. On small streams, such as at Churchill, the problem was aggravated by the activity of other mills further up the valley (as at Chipping Norton) so it was necessary to build up a substantial head of water in the millpond until there was sufficient to release through sluice gates and keep the millwheel turning. Even then the flour tended to be coarse 'grist' rather than fine flour suitable for making good bread.

---

26  *Geology of Oxford and the Valley of the Thames*, p.51.

27  Although, oddly enough, it was accidentally transferred to another Churchill – the one in Worcestershire – in Arthur Mee's *Worcestershire*, page 48, in the County Series.

Harry Phipps, the miller during the earlier part of the nineteenth century, diversified by being also a baker. In 1817 Harry Phipps came before the Oxfordshire Quarter Sessions and was fined twenty shillings for using false weights – a common form of dishonesty at that time. Following his overall policy of rebuilding his tenants' property in a solid, satisfactory and pleasing style, James Haughton Langston built a separate Miller's House for Harry Phipps. At this time, the mill seems to have been a substantial T-shaped building, with the new miller's house opposite, and an associated group of barns and stables. It may have been at this time too that the mill acquired a 'luccam` projecting from the front to facilitate elevating sacks of grain. Luccams are rare in Oxfordshire: they are strongly constructed and equipped with a pulley wheel and tackle, a roof and a small entrance doorway into the mill. Harry Phipps died in 1841 and his gravestone may still be seen in the churchyard. His work as miller and baker was taken over by his widow, Hannah. But milling was, at best, a seasonal occupation, and the need to diversify in this way by adding another cash business to milling became more pressing after the opening of the railway in 1854 that gave farmers access to the new steam-powered mills that were springing up along the line. In Kingham, the miller family of Baggs diversified by becoming beer retailers, thereby beginning the process by which Kingham Mill ultimately became a hotel.

By 1853 the miller of Churchill was James Taylor, who described himself in the street Directory as 'farmer and miller'. He, too, became the village baker. The construction of the 'Sarsden Siding' on the new branch line to Chipping Norton meant that farmers had even easier access to the steam mills such as Matthews's at Shipton-under-Wychwood. The coming of the railway also had its effect on the working of Churchill Mill, because it enabled the miller to supplement an often inadequate supply of water-power by a small steam engine which could be used in times of drought. But in the long run, the coming of the railway was the death-knell of water-mills that were first relegated to grinding grist for animal feed, and then fell into disuse.

The new tenant in 1860 was William Williams, born in Little Rollright in 1814 where his father was the miller. In the 1861 census, William and Hannah Williams had three children, of whom the youngest, Lucy, was born at Churchill mill. Hannah Williams's 19-year old brother, Stephen Wyatt, had come from his father's mill at Todenham to be apprenticed to William Williams, and the family was able to afford two resident servants: Mary Luckett who looked after the bakery, and Ann Harris who helped in the house. By the 1871 census William Williams is recorded as 'miller and farmer of thirty-eight acres employing four men and one boy'. His family had increased to seven children, all 'scholars', for whom he employed Eleanor O'Connor as a governess and teacher. To complete the complement of the mill there were two other resident servants: Martha Tarrans aged 18 and Thomas Hobbs the farm-boy. Three of the men whom Williams employed must have been labourers from the village, but the fourth, William Salma, who also lived in the village, acted both as a baker and labourer. So, in the 1870s there were twelve people living in the Miller's House, and four other families in the village who earned their living at the Mill and the Mill farm. The mid-nineteenth century must have been the time of greatest prosperity and activity at the mill. The millers, of course, were still tenants of the Sarsden Estate, now owned by Lord and Lady Ducie.

William Williams retired in about 1885 when he was 71 and died in 1901. His place was taken by his son, Edward William Williams, known as 'Noggy', who was aged about 29 when he took over the mill. Noggy Williams employed a small portable steam-engine that was stationed in the mill-yard and had a belt to drive a pulley wheel inserted in the wall of the mill. This engine was also used as a threshing machine, since Williams was also a farmer. The late Mr David Crudge remembered that there used to be a pulley wheel, about 4 – 5 feet in diameter and about six inches wide, about one third of the way up the wall above the mill leet. This pulley wheel can be plainly seen on an old picture postcard of Sarsden.

This was the period of sharp decline in the fortunes of the mill. In the 1891 census, there were only four residents in the mill-house: [Edward] William Williams, unmarried; his aunt, Sarah Wyatt, housekeeper; one house-servant, Lizzie Holtom, and William Hencher, a journeyman miller. Those who remembered him said that Noggy Williams was a short, stout man with a taciturn and intractable manner. When he caught boys from the village or from Kingham Hill scrumping apples from his orchard, he pitched them face downwards into a bed of stinging nettles and then let them take the apples home. No doubt his reputation was an incentive rather than a deterrent to any self-respecting boy. He had no children of his own, of course.

According to Mr A. Betteridge of Churchill, who still remembered the last miller, the use of the portable steam engine was the indirect cause of the closure of the mill. Charles Edward Baring Young, the squire of Daylesford, had been busy building his Boys' Homes on Kingham Hill. In 1888 he purchased Kingham Field Farm, thus extending his property to the north bank of the stream close to the mill. He converted Kingham Field Farmhouse into a residential boys' home, and needed a reliable supply of coal and other necessities that could be delivered to the siding on the railway. To facilitate this, he constructed the new private road that linked Field Farm with the siding. This created a new situation at the mill, since horse-drawn traffic now had to pass through the miller's yard and up the hill to the Homes. The story goes – and it is entirely credible – that Squire Young had a load of coal that he was waiting to fetch from the siding, but Noggy Williams was operating his threshing machine in the mill yard. When requested (probably in a peremptory manner) by Arthur Roper, Squire Young's brash cockney 'labour-master', to make way for the coal cart, Noggy flatly refused to shift his threshing machine to let the wagon past. Squire Young, although a benevolent man, was autocratic and unused to encountering opposition, so it may well have been an accumulation of incidents such as this that convinced him that the only solution was to round off his Kingham Hill estate by purchasing the mill from Lord Ducie at Sarsden.

In 1897, the Earl of Ducie sold Churchill Mill to Charles Edward Baring Young for £3,800. The sum seems excessive in comparison with Squire Young's previous purchases, for in 1888 he had purchased the whole of Kingham Field Farm, with its excellent newly-built homestead of Holwell House, and all the adjacent farm buildings, for £3,600. Kingham Field Farm was 180 acres; the Churchill Mill estate was less than twenty acres, and by 1897 the commercial value of the mill had become negligible.

Squire Young had no intention of operating the mill; he already had his own steam-powered mill on the Hill. We can only assume that he purchased the mill in order to obtain undisputed access to the sidings that would shortly become Sarsden Halt. Noggy Williams moved up the hill to Grange Farm, Churchill, where he died in 1913.

The machinery remained silent at the disused mill. Sadly, travellers by train, unwontedly stopping Adlestrop-fashion at the Halt would never again have the pleasure of hearing the millwheel turning, and listening to the soothing splash of falling water. Small boys were tempted to slip into the deserted building and set the machinery in motion, but if they did – as Arthur Roper's son Charles discovered on his way home from school in Churchill – the sound of the mill-wheel turning quickly alerted the signalman from the siding, who would come running to catch the miscreant: if mill machinery is set in motion without a supply of grain, there is a serious danger of fire.

After the Second World War, the Kingham Hill Trust started to reconstruct the mill and spent about £200 on re-roofing the building in slate. From 1952, the mill was very successfully used for pig-breeding and poultry, and in 1969 the mill was again converted into a base for Guide Camps that were held on The Hams, three at a time, during the summer. In May 1980, Kingham Hill Trust applied for planning permission to convert the mill into a private house. This was successfully completed and the house was sold into private ownership in 1981. At the same time, the Kingham Hill Trust began to evict former employees who had previously been permitted to remain in their houses, rent and rate free. These properties, including the miller's house, were also then sold.

For many years, Churchill Mill played a vital part in the village economy, and the miller took his place, second only to the vicar, at the head of the social pyramid. During the eighteenth and early nineteenth centuries water-mills flourished as agriculture became more productive, and the miller prospered. But the coming of the railway and the agricultural recession after 1873 signalled the end of water milling. Even had Squire Young not bought and closed down the mill in 1897, there would have been no future for water milling in Churchill, or anywhere else. In the village the mill was forgotten so quickly that by the mid-twentieth century it was referred to in conversation and even in print as 'Sarsden Mill' because it was situated near Sarsden Halt. But a proper understanding of the mill and of its significance in the life of the community is an essential element in the story of Churchill[28].

*Sarsden Lodge Farm*

28  I am grateful for the help of the late Mr Wilf Foreman for his wisdom and advice about Churchill Mill.

# THE RAILWAY

The network of railway lines that criss-crossed Britain in the nineteenth century not only revolutionised transport but also transformed the character of the villages along their routes. The first line – it was then still called a railroad – planned to pass through Churchill was William James's extension of his Stratford to Moreton tramway by continuing it towards London. James carefully surveyed the area south of Moreton-in-Marsh, and in the Oxfordshire County Record Office there is deposited an excellent map or section of the proposed route from Moreton-in-Marsh to Shipton-under-Wychwood. The line was to have entered the parish of Churchill almost due east of Kingham Church. From there its route is easy to trace across the fields to the Churchill Road just north of Rynehill Farm (which is marked, but not named, on the map); thence it went south-west to cross the Lyneham Road just north of Sarsden Lodge until it reached the village of Lyneham. This route runs almost parallel to the one later chosen for the Oxford, Worcester and Wolverhampton Railway. Of course the tramway was never constructed, but by surveying the ownership and occupation of the land and fields James must have raised anxiety and expectations among the villagers.

It was not until the Great Western Railway had felt its way north to Oxford that fierce competition broke out to find a route from the West Midlands to London. The initiative came entirely from the manufacturers of the Midlands and specifically, in this case, from Wolverhampton. The addition of the name 'Oxford' to the Oxford, Worcester and Wolverhampton Railway Company was to attract the interest of the Great Western in Oxford, and specifically of Isambard Kingdom Brunel who became the engineer of the OW&WR. The company was authorised by Act of Parliament in 1845, but surveys had already been carried out to find a suitable route over the northern end of the Cotswolds and the

Section Book that accompanied the Act showed the land ownership on the route selected. 1845 was a year when the railway mania in England was at its height. In that year there were one hundred and nineteen separate Acts of Parliament relating to railways and this constituted more than half of the total local legislation during that year.

Owing to the financial troubles of the OW&WR, construction was delayed for several years, but in January 1851 the company entered agreements with the contracting firm of Peto and Betts and the smaller firm of William Tredwell. At once, armies of navvies began work on the line, and reports began to flow into the local press. The inhabitants of the towns and villages on the route were unsure whether to welcome the advent of civilised transport or to fear the uncivilised army of workmen drawn from every county in England, and some from Ireland or overseas. Hard-working, highly-paid, rough living and heavy drinking, the navvies aroused admiration and fear in equal measures in the locality. Edward Lockwood, son of the Rector of Kingham, wrote[29]

> *'The railroad … was being constructed, and hundreds of navvies found a lodging here. They were a strange, rough lot, such as one might expect to meet in a new gold or diamond field abroad. The village constables were powerless to stop any disturbance which they chose to make, and our chief safety lay in their getting high wages for piece-work, so, as a rule, most of their buoyant spirits were consumed in a praiseworthy direction. But when the snow lay deep upon the ground in Winter and work was stopped, they passed most of their time in the public houses, from which they would at length emerge well primed for mischief'.*

Edward Lockwood had personal experience of the navvies when on such a snowy night a party of navvies made a frontal attack on Kingham Rectory. The Rector, aided by his two teenage sons (including Edward), charged the leading navvy down the front steps of the Rectory, using an oaken hatstand as a battering ram. But when the navvies began to threaten further violence,

---

29  *The Early Days of Marlborough College*, London, 1893, p.52.

*'I flew upstairs, and in less than no time handed my father the loaded gun which he always kept in his bedroom in those troubled times. Then the navvies … prudently withdrew'.*

The policy of these contractors was not to provide carriages, tents or lineside huts to accommodate their workmen, but to expect them to find their own lodgings in the village. It is interesting to compare the number of illegitimate babies baptised in Churchill with those baptised in Kingham for the same period. Whereas Kingham showed a substantial increase in the decade 1851-1860, there was no change in the figures for Churchill – six illegitimate births in each of the decades 1841-50, 1851-1860, 1861-1870, by comparison with eight overall in the decades 1801-1870. Evidently Kingham suffered more than Churchill from the unwanted attention of the navvies.

The chosen route brought the railway into Churchill parish close to Standbow Bridge and continued north almost entirely in the same parish until it reached the small Swail Brook that separated Churchill from Kingham. Subsequently, when the station was built, at first called Chipping Norton Junction but in 1909 renamed Kingham Station, it was (and still is) in the parish of Churchill and so rightly should have been called Churchill Station, but as there was already a Churchill on the O.W.& W.R. line in Worcestershire, it was sensible to avoid confusion. The line was officially opened to traffic on Saturday, 4th June 1853, but there was as yet no station in either Kingham or Churchill: the timetable listed stations at Ascott, Shipton, Addlestrop (sic) and Moreton.

The manufacturers of Chipping Norton, led by William Bliss of the Tweed Mill, were affronted that the OW&WR. had by-passed their town, and from 1847 began a campaign to obtain access to the railway preferably by a branch line, but certainly by the provision of a station at Kingham (or Bledington). For several years their efforts were fruitless, but in 1853 William Bliss, William Simkins Hitchcock and others were delighted when Samuel Morton Peto himself, who had discovered an affinity with William Bliss, offered to construct a branch line for them and to make a substantial financial contribution towards it. A subscription list was opened in August 1853 and work began in September 1854. James

Haughton Langston sold the land over which the line would pass at very little more than its agricultural value – one hopes that the tenant farmers were compensated by a reasonable adjustment of their rents. The line was four and a half miles long, and was entirely located in the parishes of Chipping Norton and Churchill. Steep gradients were avoided by following the line of the small river valley, and expensive engineering works were not undertaken. The total cost was £26,000, which was very cheap at that time. Peto provided £14,000 and the manufacturers and traders of Chipping Norton raised £12,000. The work proceeded fast, by day and night when the workings were lit by huge fires. The navvies were accommodated in Chipping Norton in lodgings or in huts provided by the contractors, and the Three Goats quickly changed its name to the Railway Inn.

The branch line to Chipping Norton was opened to passengers on Friday, 10th August 1855; goods trains had been using the route for the past two months. A special train brought Sir Morton and Lady Peto to Chipping Norton Junction, which was decorated with evergreens and banners, and a brass band played 'See the conquering hero comes'. At 12.45, the train drawn by the engine temporarily called 'Eugenie' (presumably in honour of the Empress of the French) brought the party of Directors and others on the fifteen-minute journey to Chipping Norton. William Bliss provided a grand lunch for some twenty to thirty guests in his home. A free lunch was provided for the employees at the Mill and their families. All shops were shut, the church bells rang, a fairground was opened with booths and stalls. Celebratory luncheons were provided at the Town Hall by courtesy of the landlord of the White Hart and at the Unicorn (for masons and carpenters), the Blue Boar (railwaymen and porters), the Fox (band and constables), the Blue Lion (employees of Mr Hitchman and Mr Bickerstaffe) and the King's Arms (ringers and others). Inevitably there were lengthy speeches, and the Town Hall was decorated with banners proclaiming: 'Unrestricted Commerce', 'Mr Bliss, the People's Friend' and, surprisingly, 'Extension of Education'. The guests left later in the afternoon to catch the six o'clock train back to Kingham.[30]

---

30  I am grateful to the late Peter Farmery for allowing me to use his research on the opening of the line. See also S.C.Jenkins and H.I.Quayle, *The Oxford, Worcester and Wolverhampton Railway*, (1977).

Unlike the Bourton-in-the-Water Railway, there was no Chipping Norton Railway Company. Money was raised by the issue of 2400 OW&WR shares, so really the line was an OW&WR line from the start. However, the shares were identified as 'Chipping Norton Branch Shares', the money was used exclusively to build the Chipping Norton branch and separate accounts were maintained for the operation of the line. The special financial arrangements ended in 1859, after which the OW&WR paid 4% to holders of Chipping Norton Branch shares. The OW&WR. merged with the short-lived West Midlands Railway Company, and then inevitably with the Great Western. Parliament required the company to build a road bridge (still referred to as 'The New Line Bridge') in place of the planned level crossing on the road leading from Kingham to Bledington. Under considerable pressure, they later built another road bridge on the Cornwell Road at Swailsford, with its uncomfortable approaches. There was a level crossing on the road to Kingham where a crossing-keeper's cottage was built, and, after 1893, a signal box at the sidings. Lord Ducie made a commendable effort to promote the commerce and agriculture of the area by building in 1879 the impressive Langston Arms Inn beside Kingham Station, with its own private access footbridge and by opening a market behind it later.

*Sarsden Halt (with Churchill Mill)*

The railway sidings beside the mill were used mainly for the delivery of coal and the collection of milk. From 1855, sidings at Churchill Mill were known as Sarsden Sidings, although there is at least one official reference to them as 'the sidings at Churchill'. After the opening of the Kingham Hill Homes in the 1880s, the sidings came into greater use and on 2nd July 1906 a halt was opened there called 'Sarsden Halt`, taking its name from the Sarsden Sidings and the Sarsden Signal Box (1893). It ought, of course, to have been 'Churchill Halt'. Ultimately, the line was extended to Cheltenham and Banbury, thus enabling it to be used by long-distance express trains from the north of England to the south and west. After 1859, the line to Chipping Norton was operated by two well-tank engines, one called 'Ben Jonson` and the other, informally, as 'Mrs Jonson'. The whole line was closed to passengers in 1962 and to goods traffic in 1964.[31]

---

31  I am deeply indebted to my son, John Mann, for correcting and clarifying the details in this account. For a full and definitive account of this railway, William Hemmings's first two volumes of *The Banbury and Cheltenham Railway*, Volume I, 2004, and Volume 2, Hemmings, Karau and Turner, 2004, are unparalleled, and exceptionally well illustrated.

# CANON CARTER

*Canon William Carter*
*(1822-1903]*

At the death of Charles Barter, his son-in-law, William Edward Dickson Carter succeeded him as Rector of 'Sarsden-cum-Churchill' and Rural Dean of Chipping Norton. William Carter was born in Fitchfield, Hants., to a well-established navy family from Portsmouth and Shanklin in the Isle of Wight. His father and his maternal grandfather were both Admirals in the Royal Navy. In 1846, when he was aged twenty-four, he came to Churchill to be Assistant Curate to Charles Barter responsible also for the parish of Cornwell. Charles Barter's seventh daughter, Ellen, fell in love with the new young curate, eight years her senior. Haughton House was built in Churchill for the newly-married couple. In 1852, Carter was appointed Vicar of Shipton-under-Wychwood where he remained until the death of his father-in-law in 1868. This enabled him to return to become the Rector of 'Sarsden-cum-Churchill', and to succeed Charles Barter as Rural Dean of Chipping Norton until his death on 23rd February 1903, by which time he was also an honorary Canon of Christ Church Cathedral, Official Principal of the Archdeaconry of Oxfordshire and Justice of the Peace. His place at Shipton-under-Wychwood was taken by his brother-in-law, the Revd Henry Barter. W. E. D. Carter was a High Churchman of the Oxford Movement school and installed a stone altar with an accompanying carved stone reredos and elaborate paintings on the east wall of the new church in the Gothic

Revival style. A photograph in a gilded frame shows him looking stout, stern and self-satisfied.

Unfortunately, Canon Carter was to be remembered not primarily for his work in the parish but for an action that he took in his capacity as a magistrate. In 1873 there was considerable arable unrest, and the National Agricultural Labourers Union was formed by Joseph Arch to protect the interests of the farm-workers. The Oxford District of the NALU was well-organized. A branch was formed at Churchill and Charles Pearce of Churchill played an active role in the Oxfordshire District[32]. During a strike on Crown Farm at Ascott-under-Wychwood, a large number of the wives, daughters and girl-friends of the striking labourers decided to picket a field gate to prevent two blackleg teenagers from going to work there. The boys were subjected to rude jibes and threatened with sticks. The police were called and seventeen of the women were brought before the Justices of the Peace in the so-called 'Chipping Norton Intimidation Case'. The two magistrates who heard the evidence at the Chipping Norton Magistrates' Court were the Revd Thomas Harris of Swerford and Canon W. E. D. Carter of Sarsden. Strictly speaking, the law (The Criminal Law Amendment Act) had not literally been broken, but the two magistrates decided that an example must be set to prevent further misbehaviour in those unruly times, and so they agreed to find sixteen of the women guilty and sentenced them to brief terms in the Oxford House of Correction (the women's prison). Ten of the women were sentenced to seven days, and the remaining six women to ten days hard labour. The case, that had been carefully watched by the N.A.L.U., caused an immediate national outcry. There were articles in the national press (including The Times), questions were asked in Parliament, and the (Liberal) Home Secretary called upon the (Tory) Duke of Marlborough as Lord Lieutenant of the County to make an immediate enquiry into this obvious miscarriage of justice. Even Queen Victoria, always protective where women were concerned, intervened and called for an enquiry. The Lord Lieutenant called upon the two miserable magistrates to write explaining the reasons for their

---

32 *Agricultural Trade Unionism in Oxfordshire, 1872-1881,* ed. Pamela Horn, ORS Vol. XLVIII, 1974.

action, and Canon Carter had to write an unctuous letter of justification, exonerating himself, and throwing the blame chiefly on Thomas Harris. By this time ten of the women had already been released, and the remaining six were brought back to Ascott in triumph by the N.A.L.U. The women were granted a royal pardon, the N.A.L.U. gave each of them a blue silk dress, and the Queen more sensibly provided them with red woollen petticoats. The Chipping Norton Intimidation Case, as it became known, led to such heavy criticism of clergy magistrates that the custom of appointing ordained men to the bench was gradually discontinued over the next thirty years and the law regarding peaceful picketing during a strike was changed. A mythology of fanciful legend grew up about the Ascott Women, and the events were given a re-enactment a century later.

Throughout the nineteenth century the Churchill village schools flourished. Early in the nineteenth century, young John Laskey arrived from Devon and opened a fee-paying school operating 'upon Dr Bell's improved system of education', beginning with 'the principles of the Christian Religion as professed by the Established Church'. In addition to the three R's, he taught mensuration, geography and English Grammar. In 1818, he made an attempt to receive boarding pupils at £16 a term, with £1 10s extra for washing. The experiment did not succeed and John Laskey moved to Kingham where he opened a highly successful grocery business in what later became Kingham Stores. At his death, he endowed a handsome charity for the poor.

By the middle of the century there were three thriving schools in the parish, staffed by competent and respectable teachers. The boys' school originally set up by Viscountess Harcourt, was re-endowed by the will of Henrietta Maria Langston in 1844. For twenty years some eighty boys were taught by Jeremiah Beezley. During the winter the school was open in the evenings as a Reading Room, providing warmth, light and information for those who did not wish (or could not afford) to spend the time in the Chequers. Two nights a week Mr Beezley gave free instruction in writing and arithmetic to adults. Apparently he also taught the daughters of Squire Langston. He died in 1856 and was succeeded by George Orford who remained for forty-five years.

Mr W. H. Anson, who contributed his reminiscences to Mrs Rose's book, was schoolmaster until his retirement.

Anne Walter's Girls' School was taught by Rochdale-bred Alice Howorth in whose memory a stained-glass window was placed in the church in 1889. There was also a Dame School for twenty infants, taught in 1851 by two Churchill ladies, Ann Butler and Rhoda Birnam.

'There are small endowments for these schools`, reported Charles Barter in 1854, 'but the chief expense is defrayed by J. H. Langston'. In 1859 and 1866 new school buildings for girls and boys were provided by J. H. Langston and his widow, Lady Julia. The original building of Anne Walter's School continued to be used for infants. The Anne Walter Trust and the Henrietta Maria Langston Trust were combined in 1994 to provide grants towards education for the children of Churchill and Sarsden.

When the Carters came to Sarsden in 1868, Ellen Carter was returning to the Rectory where she had been born in 1830. Of her eight children,

*Interior of school*

only two were boys: William Collingwood Carter who succeeded his uncle, Henry Barter, as Vicar of Shipton-under-Wychwood, was Rector of Cornwell 1889-1903, and followed his father as Rural Dean of Chipping Norton in 1903. Archibald Thomas Carter, born in 1854, became a Captain in the Royal Navy and died at Ryde on 30th November 1899. Canon Carter presented the land upon which St Paul's Church at Shanklin was built.

# THE CHURCH IN THE TWENTIETH CENTURY

After the death of Lady Julia Frances Langston, daughter of the 1st Earl of Ducie and the widow of J. H. Langston, the Sarsden estate was inherited by their daughter who had married the 3rd Earl of Ducie. Their son, Lord Moreton, administered the estate on behalf of his father, and is commemorated by Lord Moreton's Seat, with its magnificent view of Sarsden. His sister, Lady Eversleigh, inherited the estate and in 1922 it was put up for sale. Most of the tenant farmers were given first option to buy their farms at a very reasonable valuation. This sale resulted in the most extensive change in land ownership since the Enclosure Award.

When Canon Carter died in 1903, the Earl of Ducie offered the living to the Revd Edmund J. F. Johnson who was at that time the Vicar of Hillesley in Gloucestershire. Edmund Johnson came from an old Leicester family and had been educated at Oakham School and at St John's College, Cambridge. He married while he was serving his curacy at Bishopsteignton in Devon, his wife being closely related to Prebendary Wilson Carlisle, the founder of the Church Army. His brother-in-law, the Revd Edward Mosley, became Rector of Tortworth where the Ducie family had their ancestral seat and thus Lord Ducie came to know Edmund Johnson personally. At first, Edmund Johnson was disconcerted to find Sarsden Rectory so large – eighteen bedrooms and no bathroom. Moreover, Mrs Carter, Canon Carter's widow, showed a marked disinclination to leave the house which had been her home for most of her long life. But the Bishop urged Edmund Johnson to accept the nomination, and his wife was longing for a change, and so in due course the Johnson family moved to Sarsden. Canon Carter had been a High Churchman, but Edmund Johnson was Low Church and unaccustomed to the vestments and ritual that his predecessor had introduced. Nevertheless, he consented to accommodate to the customs of the parish, but commented 'I shall talk to God just the same, whatever I am wearing!' He was uneasy that his style of ministry differed from that of Canon Carter. After a few months, when he was sitting in his study deep in thought, he 'saw' Canon Carter sitting opposite him and they 'shook hands'; his mind was put at rest.

A man of gentle humour, with a deep personal faith, Edmund Johnson soon won the affection of his parishioners. It was his custom to walk round the village every afternoon to get to know his people. The Johnsons were concerned at the social conditions in the village – the poverty and drunkenness they encountered both in Churchill and locally in Oxfordshire and Gloucestershire. They welcomed contact with the villagers, practising hospitality in the Rectory and giving out bags of coal at Christmas. Mrs Johnson held sewing sessions for the wives, and the rector took The Pledge (of total abstinence) to set an example to their husbands.

Life in the Rectory was strict: no smoking or drinking was permitted, and no alcohol was served, even at his daughters' weddings. Whereas the close relationship with Sarsden House had ended with the death of Canon Carter, Mrs Johnson had social pretensions and took her daughters visiting to the homes of the local gentry – Shipton Court, Chastleton House and Bruern Abbey, and to Oxford for Eights Week. The Johnsons installed a bathroom in the Rectory, but the house was still lit by oil lamps and candles and of course there was no central heating. For transport they relied on a pony-cart and a dog-cart, and Edmund Johnson rode a tricycle, but never drove a car. There were two tennis courts at Sarsden and croquet was played there.

Edmund Johnson's ministry was evangelical, and his sermons were thoughtful and illustrated with homely anecdotes designed to appeal to his listeners and to elicit a response of faith. His daughter said of him that, if one heard him say in his inimitable way 'the peace of God which passeth all understanding', one felt that he really did understand. When he went to Sarsden church he prepared two sermons – one to use if Lord Ducie and the gentry from Sarsden House were there, or a simpler one if only the villagers attended.

Edmund Johnson stayed at Sarsden and Churchill for nearly twenty years, and saw three of his four daughters married here. He also saw the effects of the 1914-1918 War on his parishioners, as well as the onset of secularism. In a simple set of verses that he sent to his daughter Aline during the war he described a typical Sunday in January and how he rejoiced at Morning Prayer at Churchill.

> *For fifty others sang their best*
> *    With me the Psalms and Hymns,*
> *And choir boys with all the rest –*
> *    The bells were rung by Timms.*

These verses incidentally reveal the decline in church attendance in the half century since Charles Barter had made his Visitation Return in 1854. Edmund Johnson was thankful that there were fifty at Morning Prayer at Churchill, nineteen at Sarsden in the afternoon, and eighty for Evening Prayer at Churchill again at six o'clock.

Seventy men from Churchill served in the armed forces during the Great War, named by Mrs L. Rose[33] and eleven men gave their lives[34] commemorated by the memorial, made by local masons from local stone, that stands at the entrance to the village.

When he came to Churchill in 1903, Edmund Johnson was forty-seven years old. He remained here until he retired to Warsash in Hampshire in 1922, where he died eleven years later. His ministry marked the transition from the 'squarson' who was essentially one of the land-owning gentry, to the pastoral ministry of a trained parish priest.

After his retirement, the rector for the next twenty years was the Revd Martin Spearing, a scholar and a shy, quiet bachelor, whose custom was to visit every dwelling in his parishes once every year. To commemorate the centenary of All Saints Church in 1927, the original 'Squire's Pew' behind the choir stalls on the north side was replaced by a Lady Chapel.

---

33   *op. cit.* pp 76 – 77.

34   *idem* p. 70.

The communion table was made by Sam Groves of Milton-under-Wychwood.

Mr Spearing's ministry as Rector included the years of the Second World War. He retired in 1945 and died later in Brighton. He was succeeded, briefly, by the Revd S. H. Newton who found it hard to adjust to country ways after an energetic ministry in London. The parishioners believed that he referred to them as 'turnips'.

In 1948 the Revd Arthur Holmes came to Churchill with his wife, Margaret, and four young children; two more were born here. He found that there was much to be done in the parishes, and during the next fifteen years he tackled the accumulated effects of neglect and decay. The old church in the graveyard was restored again, and recalled into use for Holy Communion once a month after Mrs L. Rose had provided a new altar-rail. The graveyard was further extended and a new lychgate was dedicated by the Bishop of Dorchester in July 1953. In the following years, moving the mounds and footstones in the churchyard was a major operation.

After the war, Churchill was seriously depleted. One effect of the 1944 Education Act was that children over eleven now had to be educated in a separate secondary school. The Oxfordshire Education Committee decided to close the junior department at Churchill and provided transport to Kingham for those aged 10 – 11 years. The Infants School at Churchill was kept open, but in 1948 the headmistress, Mrs Blake, had only eight pupils. Mr Holmes and the village fought successfully to have housing for two teachers, and the endowments were still available. Of course, the buildings and facilities had to be brought up-to-date to meet the requirements of the Ministry of Education, but Sarsden-cum-Churchill Church of England Primary School achieved 'Aided' status, and the modernised buildings were rededicated by Bishop Harry Carpenter of Oxford. After the closure of the church schools in Fifield and Idbury in the 1960s, Churchill enjoyed an Indian Summer under its headmaster, Mr Mike Cockburn.

*Upper School*

St James's Church at Sarsden was repaired at the expense of Lady Wyfold, the owner of Sarsden House. At All Saints church, the organ was restored and the bells were re-hung in 1957. The response to the bells appeal was so generous that it was at last possible to complete the peal by adding two new ones cast by Taylor's of Loughborough, which were dedicated by the Bishop of Oxford on 9th May 1957. At All Saints, there were three services every Sunday and an afternoon service at Sarsden.

The Revd Arthur Holmes remembered Walter Carter, who attended all these services, a dear old man who pumped the organ at Sarsden and was sometimes referred to as 'Amen Carter' as he was a lusty one for the responses. In the 1950s and 1960s television began to have its effect on attendance at Evensong. One day, as they were hoping that one or two more might turn up, Walter Carter said: 'You know what it is, Rector? Why they won't come? It's them 'wots-its' [television aerials] on the chimneys.' Mr Holmes also remembered Mr Ernest Payne, a most faithful person, who was Churchwarden and Treasurer, a member of the choir, and did every sort of skilled and unskilled work on the church and school.

The old Sarsden Rectory had been sold after Mr Johnson retired, and a new Rectory was built on the Sarsden Road in 1924, closer to Churchill village, and designed to meet the more modest demands of modern clergy. At the Rectory, Mr Holmes kept hens, pigs, geese, ducks and bees. Water, however, was still a problem, and in dry summers had to be carried to the rectory in buckets from the village. It was not until the 1960s that the people of Churchill were at last provided with piped water.

The Revd Paul le Sueur was the last Rector of Sarsden-cum-Churchill as a separate benefice. Ordained in 1962, he served a curacy at Witney before being presented to Churchill in 1969 by the patron, Lady Wyfold. The P.C.C. had advertised the vacancy in the Church Times as having 'above average stipend' and the 250-odd applicants included two former bishops and an archdeacon. However, the parish wanted a younger man, and welcomed the 30-year old Rector with his wife, Gillian, and two daughters. The le Sueurs took an instant liking to the village, with its compact group of church, school, inn, shop, garage and village hall. At that time, Dick Rose and his sister-in-law, Mrs Sheila Rose, were the Churchwardens, Arthur Bryant the Reader, Horace Hoverd and his sister Mollie Captains of the Tower and stalwarts in the choir. At first, services were poorly attended: eight or nine came to the eight o'clock Holy Communion at Churchill; three or four at Sarsden at 9.30. There were about fifteen at Matins at 11 a.m. and half a dozen at Evening Prayer at 6 p.m.

During their five years at Churchill (1969-1974) Paul and Gill le Sueur brought fresh life into the parish. Gill found a set of hand bells in the tower, and trained a team of girl ringers – a tradition continued by Mrs Isabel Harman – and also ran a Sunday School in the Ann Walter Hall. The old church in the graveyard was still used for funerals and for an annual communion service on All Souls' Day.

Looking back, Paul le Sueur remembered the Rectory, with its vegetable patch ploughed up by Tony Rose and enriched by an annual delivery of farmyard manure; the stray dog, Bonnie, whom they adopted, and who once, being shut into the churchyard before a service, kept the entire congregation at bay outside the gate; the inexorable tyranny of the six harvest festival services each year; the thief who stole the cross and candlesticks from the altar, and who was caught more than two years later in possession of more than two hundred items from other churches – but not those from Churchill; waiting with his confirmation class to watch the Heythrop Hunt go by, and, after the last horseman had passed, seeing the fox leisurely cross the road; the lively village school under the progressive headship of Mr M.E.Cockburn, and the old-world courtesy and friendship of the parishioners.

The most memorable achievement of those years was the restoration of All Saints tower. No work had apparently been done on the tower since 1826, and to make matters worse the stone had been secured with iron ties that had rusted and caused expansion. An appeal was launched, sponsored by Lady Wyfold and supported by Sir John Betjeman who wrote:

*It is a beautiful landmark and has ... been an eye-catcher for miles around, and a delightful one. I am sure it was built with this object in view. Although the style is English Perpendicular Gothic, the Tower is in the great tradition of English landscape gardening. Its disappearance would be a grave loss to a rolling wooded landscape.*

When the Revd Paul le Sueur resigned in 1974 to move to Clifton Hampden, the Revd Roger Morgan, already Rector of Kingham and Daylesford, succeeded him. This was part of the diocesan scheme for pastoral reorganisation, bringing together the four parishes into one benefice. By Order in Council dated 19th December 1979, the benefice of Sarsden with Churchill was united with the benefice of Kingham and Daylesford. This order specifically stated that 'the parishes shall continue distinct,' and therefore, contrary to current usage, the incumbent was still, strictly speaking, the Vicar of Churchill and the Rector of Sarsden, although he derived his formal title of Rector from the other three parishes in the living. The association of the four parishes involved a reorganisation in the pattern of services, and the introduction of combined benefice services in Kingham and

Churchill. Although it was hard for parishioners to overcome traditional loyalty, those who ventured across the parish boundaries found new friendships, and the large numbers attending the united services were a great encouragement. It was therefore a disappointment when the Diocese sold the Rectory in Churchill, and the Morgans moved back to Kingham. The Revd Roger Morgan resigned in 1978 to become Vicar of St Cuthbert's, West Hampstead, and he was succeeded by the Revd Nigel Bennett from 1979 to 1985. When he resigned to become Chaplain of the Bluecoat School, Reading, the Revd David Arthur Streater was inducted on 15th July 1986.

# THE METHODIST CHAPEL

In his account of the new Methodist Chapel, the late Mr David Crudge rightly identified two factors that weakened the old semi-feudal social order in the village. The first was the coming of the railway and the inevitable influence of the new railway town of Swindon. The Regent Street Primitive Methodist Church in Swindon took an active interest in promoting dissent, and along the route of the Oxford, Worcester & Wolverhampton railway a number of nonconformist chapels – Primitive, Wesleyan, Baptist, Congregationalist and undenominational – began to appear to meet the moral and spiritual needs of the navvies, railway employees and the working class inhabitants of the villages through which the line passed. One of these was the undenominational chapel at Kingham (1851), later to become Wesleyan, and another was the Primitive Methodist Chapel at Churchill (1852). By 1924, this chapel had become dilapidated and had not been in use for several years, but the surviving members of the Society continued to meet in the cottage owned by a Local Preacher, Mr W. Peachey, and, after his death, of his widow.

The second factor, Mr Crudge explained, was the great agricultural depression at the end of the nineteenth century, caused largely by cheap shipments of grain coming in from North America. Farms on the Sarsden Estate became vacant as the tenants could no longer afford to stay, and land became neglected. A few landlords, including the Sarsden Estate, let their farms to West Country farmers who were more used to stock farming and therefore able to survive. Many of them came into this area, and some of them were Methodists. Dairy farming was better able to weather the depression because the railways were able to transport milk in churns direct to the great cities. The milk train left Sarsden Halt every weekday shortly after 7 a.m. As work became scarce after the 1880s, unemployed labourers were evicted or decided to migrate to the cities or to the U.S.A., Canada, Australia, New Zealand and Brazil. The early Primitive Methodists in Churchill had consisted almost entirely of agricultural labourers.

One of the West Country farmers who took up the tenancy of Churchill Farm was Mr J. B. Crudge from Barton Farm, Lapford, Devon. The Sarsden Estate had been inherited in 1863 by the Earl of Ducie who had married Julia, daughter of James Haughton Langston. Their son, Henry John Reynolds, Earl of Ducie, died on 28th October 1921, and his long and complex will was proved on 18th May 1922. The Sarsden Estate was inherited by Trustees on behalf of his daughter, Constance Emily, Baroness Eversley. The family relationships were particularly complicated, and the document which established the right of the Trustees to sell the land on behalf of Lady Eversley ran to twenty-six typescript pages of approximately A3 size. Effectively, this enabled existing tenant farmers to purchase the freehold of their land on reasonable terms. Churchill Farm, 260 acres 1 rood and 31 perches, was sold to Mr Herbert James Crudge on 5th December 1922 for £5,100.

It had been one of the dearest wishes of Mr Crudge that a new Primitive Methodist Chapel should be erected in the village. Sadly, Mr Crudge died on 22nd November 1924, leaving a young family and a widow, Edith Ada Crudge, to run the farm. Mrs Crudge took the initiative in proposing the new chapel, and made a start by offering a prime site for it adjoining Churchill Farm on the Kingham Road. All the former Trustees of the former chapel in Churchill were dead or had resigned, so a new Trust was set up on 7th April 1926 consisting of eleven members including Mrs Crudge and Mr George Bernard Crudge of Conduit Farm. The other Trustees included a cowman, a labourer, a hawker, a yard foreman, a wheelwright, a van man, a Co-op employee and a plumber's mate. Apart from the Crudges, only one other Trustee, Alfred Henry Pearce, was resident in Churchill. Fred Pearce provided continuity with the former Methodist Chapel where his children had been baptised forty years before. The conveyance of the land for the new chapel gave the measurements as fifty-seven by seventy-eight feet. The old chapel in the village was in such disrepair that it was sold to Mr G.B. Crudge for

£10, which enabled them to pay off the remaining balance of unpaid mortgage and the legal fees.

Mrs Crudge gave the site of the new chapel, worth £30, and paid for the stone and haulage to the site (£40); the stone was brought from Mr Hobbs's quarry at Chadlington. Mr W. G. Eaton, an architect from Witney, drew up the plans for the building and donated his fees (£40) to the building fund. The twenty-three foundation stones were laid on Saturday 2nd October 1926. Mr David Crudge, then aged four, distinctly remembered laying a stone in memory of the orphaned children of the late H.J.Crudge. The formal opening took place on Easter Day, 18th April 1927, and Richard Cadbury, the chocolate manufacturer and a Quaker who knew Mrs Crudge personally, presided. After the service there was a tea in the village Schoolroom, and then so many attended for an evening service that it had to be held in an adjacent field.

On 20th January 1928, Churchill Methodist Chapel received the official certificate for it to be used as 'a Place of Meeting for Religious Worship by a Congregation or Assembly of persons calling themselves Primitive Methodists'. It was not until 1946 that the church applied for registration of the solemnization of marriages, and the first couple to be married there were Alfred Rutland and Alice Watkins.

Five years after the chapel was built, the long-awaited Methodist union took place. Distons Lane (Primitive Methodist) chapel in Chipping Norton was closed and Churchill became part of the Chipping Norton united Methodist Circuit in the Oxford District. The two traditions, Primitive and Wesleyan, had co-existed throughout the nineteenth century; they were now united. Significantly for Churchill, union enabled them to establish closer relations with the Wesleyan Chapel in Kingham, and the two congregations were able to meet together on a friendly basis.

In 1931, electric lighting was installed, and in 1960 electric heating was provided instead of the old coke-burning stove. Once during the Second World War, presumably in 1944, the chapel was filled to capacity by American servicemen when their Methodist chaplain conducted a communion service prior to their embarkation for the continent. On

28th June 1970, Bishop Priestley of the Church of South India preached at the morning service. Since the Church of South India unites several Protestant denominations, including Anglicans and Methodists, the parish church of All Saints cancelled its service to enable the Anglican congregation to attend the chapel. This was the beginning of what would become an increasingly friendly relationship between Anglicans and Methodists.

But 'by the 1970s`, David Crudge said, 'ordinary Sunday congregations were often disappointing. Evening services had long since been abandoned, and in 1980 it was decided to meet for worship fortnightly. On one occasion, only the preacher, the organist and one other person were present. Things looked bleak'. They looked bleak elsewhere, too. In 1986 Kingham Methodist Chapel closed. But the transference of some former Kingham Methodists to Churchill, and the unexpected arrival of several committed Methodists from the staff of Kingham Hill School led to a revival of numbers, and a major reconstruction of the chapel fabric was undertaken in 1988.

*Churchill Post Office and Chequers Inn*

In 2002, Churchill Methodist Chapel celebrated the 75th anniversary of its building. But it was also the 150th anniversary of the Primitive Methodist Society, and the 203rd anniversary of the beginning of Methodist witness in the village. This is a record they are rightly proud of.[35]

---

35 Sources: personal recollections communicated to me by David Crudge; documents in Chipping Norton Methodist Circuit Safe; the *Primitive Methodist Magazine* and the *Methodist Recorder*; the *Cotswold Journal*; Oxon CRO Pellatt XI 1/ 1-5.

# EPILOGUE

Churchill today has lost many of the facilities that formerly enabled it to be a thriving and self-sufficient community. In 1981 the population fell to 421 – the lowest ever recorded since census returns began in 1801. It no longer has a resident vicar, and has become part of the enlarged Chipping Norton benefice, with a team ministry. There are fewer farms, but those that remain are larger and well-run. The Chipping Norton branch railway line closed to passengers in 1962, but the main line still operates successfully, with Kingham Station (in Churchill parish) well patronised. Declining population, more privately-owned vehicles and the growth of supermarkets in Chipping Norton progressively reduced the need for the only remaining shop in the village, and the Village Stores closed in 1977. The Chequers, once famous for its horn-blowing competition, still flourishes but the Langston Arms has become a retirement home and the market there closed in the 1960s. The Forge, under the skilled control of Mr Williams assisted by Mr Marston, for many years operated as a petrol station and remains as a successful repair garage. The main Forge building is now a guest house. The resident policeman was withdrawn. The village primary school had to close when there were only 12 pupils left on the roll. The Methodist Chapel is still open for worship. All Saints Church survived a potentially disastrous fire in 2007. The remains of the Old Church in the graveyard have been magnificently restored and equipped as the Churchill Heritage Centre. It is a heritage worth preserving to celebrate a community that has lived, worked, struggled and survived for two thousand years.

# INDEX

Methodists, 89,126 (Primitive) 90, 92, 127

Methodist Chapel, 123, 125, 127 (and see 'Primitive Methodist')

Moore, Lady Alice, 31

Morecroft George, 97

Morecroft, George (Vicar of Kingham), 31

Morecroft,  George (son of vicar of Kingham), 26, 28, 34

Moreton, Lord, 115

Morris dancing, 55

Mortuary fees, 12

National Agricultural Labourers Union, 111

New Church, 84, 85, 88, 110, 117, 119, 128

New Church tower, 121

New Stone Age, 2

de Noers (Nowers), 6
   (Arms of), 84
   (Charter from), 8

Non-Juror, 47, 50

Norman Conquest, 5


Oakley, Thomas, 96

Oath of Abjuration, 49

Oath of Conformity, 48, 49

Oath of Protestation (1641), 29, 30

Oath of Supremacy, 47, 48, 49

Old Church, 1, 10, 28, 39, 47, 51, 56, 118, 120
   (demolition) 84
   (as mortuary chapel) 94
   (as Heritage Centre), 95

Open fields, 64
   (Commons and meadows), 66, 73
   (Enclosure), 64, 63
   (Partial Enclosure), 18


Parish registers, 28

Phillips, John, (nephew of William Smith), 78, 98

Phipps, Harry (miller), 99

Plowman, John (architect), 85

Plurality, 57

Population (Churchill), 95, 96
   (Sarsden) 95

Primitive Methodist Chapel, 92, 123


Queen Anne, 47, 48, 49

Queen Elizabeth I, 25

Queen Victoria, 111


Railway (Kingham to Chipping Norton), 83, 99, 104
   (influence of), 123

Rector of Churchill (John), 9

Rector of Sarsden, 33, 51, 87

Rectory (Churchill), 8, 122

Reformation, The, 21, 23

Repton, G.S., 83, 88, 95

Restoration, The, 33, 35

Rocks (underlying Churchill), 2

Rolle, Denys, 63, 67

Roman villa, 3

Rose, Mrs Lilian, xiv, 6, 17, 19, 26, 65, 71, 84, 117, 118

Rural Dean (of Chipping Norton), 91, 110


St Frideswide, (Priory of), 6
   (Cartulary of), 6
   Stipend of vicar of Churchill, 13
   Tithes of, 8

Sarsden,
   Cross, 13, 84
   Church, 13, 17, 56, 84, 119
   Glebe, 88
   House, 13, 39, 79, 82, 83
   Parish, 1, 53
   (Union with Churchill), 121
   Pond , 80
   Rector, 51, 56, 63
   Rectory, 91, 120
   Register, 95
   Siding, 99, 109
   Vicar's Stipend, 13

Sarsbrook, 78

Sarsgrove House, 88

School, 22, 112, 113, 118, (see 'Charity Schools')